the brown dog affair

the story of a monument that divided the nation

peter mason

Dedicated to my mother, Christine

Thanks to: Emma Hopley, John King, Eamonn Rafferty, Tony Shaw, Mike Squires, Jose Parry

Photographs used by kind permission of:
BUAV, National Monument Record, Jose Parry, University College London Library, Traci-Leigh Scarlett

Copyright © Peter Mason 1997

Published by: Two Sevens Publishing
30 Wynter Street, London SW11 2TZ

ISBN: 0 9529854 0 3

contents

the trial 7

    two Swedish campaigners ... a controversial speech ... a celebrated libel action
    ... unprecedented public interest ... the punitive verdict

the fountain 23

    genesis of the memorial ... search for a sponsor ... finding a home in radical Battersea
    ... conservative opposition ... putting it to the vote

unveiled 37

    a nervous opening ceremony ... a phoney war ... an attack on a foggy night ...
    punishment for the offenders ... national prominence for the dog once again

the 'riots' 47

    students take to the streets ... effigy burning and fights with the police
    ... a showdown in Trafalgar Square ... the dog survives unscathed

more trouble 61

    students clash with anti-vivisectionists ... mass meetings support the dog
    ... complaints about policing costs... first moves to destroy the monument

all change 75

    turnaround in Battersea ... official moves to remove dog ... a night-time
    disappearance ... indecision and a legal challenge ... an indistinct death

reborn 94

    life after the dog ... an assessment of its significance ... the class war ... renewed
    interest 70 years later... a modern day successor

chronology 112

mayors of Battersea 113

bibliography 114

index 115

introduction

AT THE CENTRE of the Latchmere Recreation Ground in the south London borough of Battersea, not far from the Latchmere pub, there is a small hump on the tarmac pavement that cuts through to Battersea Park Road.

Its contours are barely discernible from the general surrounds, but they are significant nonetheless, for they are all that remain of one of the most controversial statues ever erected in Britain.

The brown dog memorial was an unprepossessing bronze drinking fountain erected in memory of an anonymous London mongrel, but it became a national *cause célèbre* in Edwardian Britain and a focus for alternative politicians of the era. It spent most of its short life under a 24-hour police guard.

Unveiled in 1906 to commemorate a dog killed by animal experimenters at the University of London, it was loathed by the establishment not just for its bold-faced anti-vivisectionist inscription, but also for its capacity to act as a rallying point for political activists from a whole host of disparate movements. Suffragettes, trade unionists, socialists, marxists, liberals, leading figures in the temperance movement and all kinds of mavericks flocked to its defence. Many local people in Battersea adopted it as their own.

Members of the medical establishment in particular grew to hate this provocative bronze dog for the scorn it poured over their profession. When orthodox attempts to remove the memorial came to nothing, medical students and their supporters tried to smash the dog under the cover of darkness. Later they took violently to the streets in what became known as the 'brown dog riots'. Newspapers gorged themselves on the controversy, there were endless public meetings to discuss the memorial's legitimacy, and questions were asked in Parliament.

In the end, however, the brown dog's fate rested not with national politicians but with the local council – which eventually pulled the monument down in the dead of night.

The anti-vivisectionists were enraged, but they could do nothing to save the memorial. More than 85 years later, only the hump remains. Next to it, there is a sign on an iron fence. It reads 'No Dogs'.

the trial

two Swedish campaigners ... a controversial speech ... a celebrated libel action ... unprecedented public interest ... the punitive verdict

THE BROWN DOG memorial may have been born in 1906, but the courtship that led to its conception began in November 1903, when the real life animal on which the statue was based came to national prominence in a celebrated libel trial.

The four-day trial, which stimulated lively public debate over the rights and wrongs of vivisection and devoured many column inches in the national press, arose indirectly from a controversial book called *The Shambles of Science* written by two little known Swedish women, Louise Lind-af-Hageby and Leisa Schartau.

Subtitled *Extracts from the diary of two students of physiology*, the book had begun to take shape in early 1903, when Lind-af-Hageby and Schartau decided that their personal notes describing what they claimed to have seen while watching animal experiments at various London medical colleges deserved to be read by a wider audience.

Lind-af-Hageby and Schartau had known each other as children in the cosy, privileged world of upper-class Scandinavia. Lind-af-Hageby was the youngest daughter of a former chief justice of Sweden and after an education in Stockholm had studied for a time at Cheltenham Ladies College in England, while Schartau was the daughter of a captain in the Swedish army.

Although both had met on a number of occasions during their younger days, it was only in their early twenties that they had became close friends by discovering – during a chance meeting at the Stockholm Opera House in 1899 – that they had a mutual interest in science, good causes and a shared but undefined yearning to improve the world. In 1900 they decided to travel together to Paris, where the highlight of their trip was to have been a visit to the world famous Pasteur Institute, a renowned centre of medical research.

They had gone to admire the achievements of modern science, but neither had bargained for the unregulated laboratories of France, where almost any animal experiment, however unscientific or brutal, was tolerated. What they saw at the Pasteur Institute horrified them.

'We found cages upon cages, vast rooms filled with hundreds of animals that had been inoculated with diseases,' recalled Lind-af-Hageby more than a quarter of a century later. 'Now and then the young and amiable man who conducted us through the institute opened the door of a cage, took out the dead body of a rabbit or a guinea-pig and threw it into a pail under the table. To my astonished inquiry as to whether each animal that had been inoculated was not carefully studied, he replied that it was holiday time and that many of the research workers were absent.'

Lind-af-Hageby was particularly struck by the plight of one dog which tried to reach her with its paws through the bars of its cage. 'The look of suffering and intense appeal went straight to my heart, and from that moment the fate of vivisected animals became my constant concern,' she said. Schartau was similarly struck – the two young friends, now convinced beyond all doubt that vivisection was immoral and unscientific, had found their mission in life.

When they returned to Sweden the same year, both women began to immerse themselves in the fight against animal experimentation. Together in December 1900 they founded the Anti-Vivisection Society of Sweden, of which they became joint honorary secretaries in April 1901.

Determined to fight the vivisectionists on their own scientific ground, they stepped up their studies of physiology and within another year had decided they needed to move to London to extend their knowledge. Still both in their early twenties, they enrolled in the autumn of 1902 as students at the London School of Medicine for Women (now the Royal Free Hospital), where there was no animal experimentation. The school did, however, have an arrangement which allowed its students to visit medical demonstrations at other colleges throughout the capital – and both women began to take full advantage.

During their time at the women's school they attended around 100 lectures and demonstrations at various laboratories, of which 50 involved experiments on live animals and 20 could be classed as full-scale vivisection. They strove to maintain a low profile throughout, but made no secret of their identities or their views if asked, and took copious notes of what they saw.

In the end, Lind-af-Hageby and Schartau decided they had seen enough; in mid-April 1903 they gave up their degree studies in disgust. Whether this had always been their plan is a matter of contention, but Lind-af-Hageby claimed shortly afterwards that the pair had fully intended to complete their courses.

'It was not at first our intention to make our experiences public in

Left to right: Lind-af-Hageby, Coleridge, Schartau

this way; we only hoped to be able to do our work better with them,' she said. 'The idea of working for a final examination and scientific degree, which we at first held, has been given up because physiology is at present inseparable from experiments on animals, and nobody objecting to them could have any chance of obtaining a degree.'

Certainly both women appeared to have been well capable of completing their studies if they had wanted to, and even a soon-to-be arch rival admitted that they 'were regarded by the teacher of physiology at the women's school as being very advanced and intelligent students'. They must have known, however, that their course would have entailed vivisection – in fact that seems to have been precisely the reason they signed on in the first place. More likely they saw the course as a means of gathering information, and their subsequent actions suggest this was so; they enrolled at the London School of Medicine as 'partial' students, a reduced-fee status introduced for those who did not intend to pursue their studies the whole way to becoming a doctor.

On 14 April 1903, almost as soon as they had left their course, Lind-af-Hageby and Schartau took the manuscript of their diaries to Stephen Coleridge, a barrister from an establishment family historically committed to the anti-vivisection cause and the honorary secretary of the National Anti-Vivisection Society (NAVS). They read him passages from the manuscript of their diaries, which they were now planning to publish, and they talked to him about their experiences in the various medical colleges of London. Coleridge found himself drawn to their revelations in a chapter of the manuscript called *Fun*, in which the pair claimed they had witnessed distressing and largely pointless animal experiments conducted in a general atmosphere of light heartedness at the physiological lecture theatre of the University of London's University College, one of the premier centres of vivisection.

More specifically, they gave details of one particular demonstration in front of around 70 students in the late afternoon of 2 February 1903 in which a brown dog, already sporting a wound from what they presumed was a previous experiment, was cut open at the front of the neck to expose its salivary gland. The dog, which did not appear to the Swedish onlookers to have been properly anaesthetised, struggled and writhed as the demonstration took place until about half an hour later it was taken away from the lecture theatre to be killed.

Coleridge believed he saw in this account at least two possible infringements of the 1876 Cruelty to Animals Act, which his own society had helped to bring into being. First, the presence of two wounds appeared to show that the animal had been used for more than one experiment, which was illegal. Second, the dog did not seem to be sufficiently anaesthetised, – also against the law.

Despite his society's role in creating the legislation, Coleridge had little faith in the effectiveness of the Cruelty to Animals Act. Anyone wanting to bring a charge under its terms had – thanks to the related Public Authorities Act of 1898 – to do so within six months of the alleged incident, and because Lind-af-Hageby and Schartau's accounts related to events that were already almost four months distant, Coleridge had little time in which to gather sufficient supporting evidence, if indeed he could have found any. In any case, and more importantly, a prosecution under the Cruelty to Animals Act could be made only with the special approval of a largely unsympathetic home secretary – a rare occurrence at the time.

Coleridge opted instead to sidestep what more radical anti-vivisectionists believed was a deliberately obstructive law by moving the matter into the wider domain. Realising that he could at least create some valuable public relations out of the women's allegations, he decided to bring the matter to national attention by repeating their hitherto private charges in a high-profile public speech.

With the women's permission, Coleridge chose to do so on the evening of 1 May 1903 at the packed and very public annual meeting of the NAVS at St James's Hall in St James's Church, Piccadilly, London – a gathering of between 2,000 to 3,000 people described by the hostile British Medical Journal (BMJ) as 'skilfully stage managed with judicious arrangement of cast and careful preparation of effects'. Messages of support and apologies for absence were sent from various prominent figures, including the novelists Jerome K Jerome, Thomas Hardy and Rudyard Kipling.

Speaking to an expectant meeting chaired by Lord Llangattock, the society's president, Coleridge proposed a resolution that the 'cowardly, immoral and detestable' act of vivisection should be banned. During his speech he read out a short statement from Lind-af-Hageby – whom he described only as an anonymous 'eyewitness' and did not identify even by sex. The statement, which had been endorsed privately by Schartau, gave a first public airing to the brown dog incident, which the two women had discussed with Coleridge two weeks earlier. More importantly, it named Dr William Bayliss, assistant professor of physiology at University College, as the man who had conducted the experiment.

The dog, Coleridge told his audience, was brought to the lecture theatre through a door to a back-room caging area from which Lind-af-Hageby heard, as the door swung open, 'long drawn howling and whining like that of dogs in terror and agony'. The animal, 'a big brown dog of the terrier type,' was stretched on its back on an operation board, its legs fixed to the board, its mouth tightly muzzled so it could make no noise, and its head held firmly in a specially designed head-holder.

'In the skin of the abdomen there were several scarcely healed scars and wounds; in one of them that seemed to be rather fresh there was left a pair of clamping forceps,' read out Coleridge. 'It was evidently not the first time that this dog had had to serve science.'

Bayliss, claimed the eyewitness, then opened the dog's neck ready for electrical stimulation, but the dog 'struggled forcibly during the whole experiment and seemed to suffer extremely during the stimulation. No anaesthetic had been administered in my presence and the lecturer said nothing about any attempts to anaesthetise the animal having previously been made. The 'violent and purposeful' struggles of the dog 'indicated complete consciousness' throughout its half-hour ordeal.

Naming Bayliss as the perpetrator of such deeds was virtually guaranteed to ensure some kind of challenge in the courts, but just to make certain, Coleridge added some florid comments of his own. Through the University College portals, he said, 'there passes a never-ending procession of helpless dumb creatures. Dogs lost or stolen from their homes where they had known nothing but affection follow one another down that Via Dolorosa into a scene of nameless horror, where man degrades his race and his manhood and brings upon that university a smirch that time itself will never erase'. Lind-af-Hageby's statement, he said, was enough to make the blood run cold. 'If this is not torture, let Mr

Bayliss and his friends ... tell us in heaven's name what torture is'.

Warming to his theme, and to the accompaniment of loud cheers, Coleridge went on to claim that 'the deep and abiding humanity of the British race' would be offended beyond measure by what was happening in such 'dens of infamy'. They would, in their 'irresistible thousands set free the victims in their cages, smash to atoms the horrible instruments of torture and leave every laboratory in the kingdom a heap of ruins.'

There was only one national newspaper reporter at the meeting – a writer from the sympathetic Daily News who had apparently been tipped off in advance by Coleridge. The reporter's verbatim report of the honorary secretary's sensational speech appeared at some length in the following morning's paper, and was picked up with relish by other national and regional newspapers during the next three days.

As the significance of the speech began to sink in, there were questions in the House of Commons on its central allegations, including a series of three inquiries during the next fortnight from Sir Frederick Banbury, the Conservative MP, who had been at the St James's Hall meeting and was sponsoring a vivisection bill aimed at abolishing animal experiments purely for demonstration to students. The Unionist home secretary Aretas Akers Douglas revealed there had been 232 experiments on dogs at University College in the year up to December 31 1902, but said he would be taking no action over the allegations. The pressure mounted on Bayliss to launch a response.

In a letter to the Daily News of 8 May 1903, Coleridge laid down the challenge unequivocally. 'As soon as Dr Bayliss likes to test the *bona fides* and accuracy of my public declaration ... he shall be confronted from the witness box by the eyewitness I rely upon,' he said. 'I hardly need say that on our side we should be very pleased to have the opportunity of interrogating Dr Bayliss on his methods in the laboratory.'

That same day, with the encouragement of the eminent surgeon Sir Victor Horsley, Bayliss instructed his solicitors to write to Coleridge asking for a full apology and a retraction of the St James's Hall statement. When the demand was ignored, a writ for libel and slander was issued on 12 May, claiming that Coleridge's statement amounted to an accusation that Bayliss had been guilty of breaking the law, that he was a cruel and inhumane torturer, and that he was therefore unfit to hold his office.

The case of Bayliss v Coleridge began before a jury on 11 November 1903 in front of Lord Chief Justice Lord Alverstone at the High Court in the Strand, London, and continued over four days until 18 November. Public interest in what the BMJ called 'a test case of the utmost gravity'

Bayliss, up front on the right, poses for a mock-up of the brown dog experiment. The photograph was used as evidence in the libel trial

was enormous: there were queues 30 yards long for the public gallery each day and the Morning Leader reported that the packed and often rowdy court 'sometimes reached almost fever heat at certain stages of the case'. Even interested barristers, said Kennel News, 'were mercilessly refused admission'. There was not a spare seat nor any standing room in the public gallery throughout the proceedings.

Interruptions and applause from the public sections continually annoyed the judge, who berated spectators on several occasions about their behaviour and warned boisterous medical students that the court was 'not a lecture theatre'. After representations from the jury, who felt they were having to cope with an unusual amount of strain, the judge agreed to pay each juror a guinea a day rather than the previously agreed guinea for the entire case. Lord Alverstone also had to warn jurors not to open any correspondence they received during the trial – he had already been sent 'a good many' anonymous letters but had put them to one side and hoped they would do likewise.

First to give evidence was Professor Ernest Starling, chair of physiology at University College, who, though not named by Coleridge in his statement, had been the man to first perform an operation on the brown dog in question. Professor Starling told the court he had initially

the trial

opened up 'a small brown mongrel allied to a terrier' on 3 December 1902 (Coleridge had said the animal was 'big') The mongrel, which had 'short roughish hair' and weighed only 14lb, had a two inch long incision cut into the wall of its abdomen so that one of its two pancreatic ducts could be tied. The experiment, he claimed, was part of research into the causes of pancreatitis (the inflammation of the pancreas) and diabetes.

After Starling's operation the dog was returned to its cage, where it was left for two months until 2 February 1903 – the day it was seen in the lecture theatre by Lind-af-Hageby and Schartau. Bayliss's counsel, Rufus Isaacs, claimed the dog had made a full recovery within ten days of his first operation and was 'quite well and running about' when he was fetched again on 2 February.

On that day Starling, working backstage of the lecture room, had once more opened up the dog's abdomen – this time with a smaller incision – for what he said was a follow-up 'experimental inspection' in the presence of Bayliss which lasted around three quarters of an hour. After observing the 'minimal' consequences of his first operation, Starling told the court he had the incision clamped with a pair of forceps. He then passed the dog over to Bayliss, who began another operation on the dog as preparation for his third spring term lecture in a course of ten presentations on 'the mechanism of the secretory process'.

Bayliss told the court he cut open the dog at the front of the neck to reveal one of the lingual nerves of the salivary glands, which he then cut and attached to electrodes. After tying tubes into the carotid artery and salivary duct he was ready for his demonstration – which he hoped would show that the pressure at which saliva was secreted was greater than blood pressure. He ordered his laboratory attendant, Charles Scuffle, to carry the dog on the operating board to the front of the house, where the students would soon be arriving.

Bayliss's demonstration was not a success. Electrical stimulation of the nerve produced little or no reaction, so that after about half an hour of futile probing the dog was taken away by Scuffle, who passed it on to an unlicensed research student named Henry Dale. Dale told the jury he took out the pancreas for microscopic examination, then killed the dog by thrusting a knife into its heart – an especially embarrassing admission for the prosecution given that Scuffle had already sworn, on oath, that Dale had actually killed the dog either with chloroform or with the anaesthetic mixture.

The Dale-Scuffle confusion must, as Lind-af-Hageby later said, 'have been rather discomforting to those who believe in the scrupulous accuracy of vivisectional observations and accounts'. Yet in the context of the case it was largely irrelevant, as was Starling's decision to hand over the dog for a third incision.

Starling was clearly in the wrong, as the Cruelty to Animals Act stipulated that once an animal had been subjected to more than one operation it should be killed 'as soon as the object of the experiment has been attained'. By failing to kill the dog after he had finished his 'experimental inspection,' he had defied the law. Even the Lancet, which had been fiercely anti-Coleridge throughout the court case, admitted after the trial that 'it may be contended that Professor Starling ... committed a technical infringement of the Act'.

Starling justified his actions by claiming he had saved a life by doing so. 'It was a question of using this dog which was to be killed ... or to take a brand new dog and kill it for this very purpose,' he said. 'It was simply a question of taking one dog instead of two.' Anti-vivisectionists were not impressed by his explanation – Lind-af-Hageby accused him of donning 'the garb of solicitude for the sacredness of animal life' – but Starling's activities were of no consequence as far as the case was concerned. He had not sued for libel, as he had not been named in Coleridge's statement. Only Bayliss's behaviour was at issue, and the rest of the case turned on the latter's responsibility for making sure the animal was properly anaesthetised.

As chief witnesses for the defence and, according to Coleridge's counsel Lawson Walton, 'young ladies of great refinement and education', Lind-af-Hageby and Schartau told the jury that, being the first arrivals in the lecture hall on 2 February, they had seen the dog in the passage ready for the demonstration. They had followed Bayliss and his attendant into the lecture room as they brought the dog in, and after a moment both men moved out of the room, leaving the women a precious two or three minutes to examine the dog alone before the arrival of about 60 other students.

Lind-af-Hageby and Schartau told the court they saw six scars on the dog's abdomen, that the animal was arching its back and jerking its legs in an effort to be free, and that they could detect no smell of ether or chloroform, nor hear the characteristic hissing sound of the anaesthesia equipment. In fact, they could not see any apparatus to bring anaesthesia to the dog, or any tubing in the dog's trachea.

Once the experiment began they clearly saw, from their seats in the third row, the dog again arch its back, 'upheave its abdomen' and tremble convulsively. The movements were 'violent and purposeful' and showed the dog was suffering. When Bayliss first approached the dog it had shown what they believed was fear.

Bayliss, who told the court he had no medical qualification but had held a licence for vivisection since 1890 and had been a teacher of physiology at the college since 1900, flatly denied nearly all of the Swedish women's claims. He showed the jury an operation board identical to the one to which the brown dog had been fixed, then argued that the 'violent and purposeful struggles' described by the women were in fact nothing more than small twitches brought on by canine chorea – a condition which induces continual involuntary jerking movements akin to St Vitus's Dance in humans.

The twitching, he said, affected 'one side of the body only, chiefly the muscles and the limbs' – a view supported by Starling, who said there were small movements in the left side arm and leg, and by a number of other students present at the lecture, including Janet Claypon, Ella Parker and Eleanor Lowry from the London School of Medicine for Women, and George Woodford and Douglas Hume from St Bartholomew's Hospital. Bayliss said he could not have conducted his experiment if the dog had been struggling, as the tubes he was using to anaesthetise it were fragile and would have broken.

The dog, Bayliss said, was knocked out earlier in the day with an injection of morphine, then anaesthetised half an hour later with six fluid ounces of a mixture of alcohol, chloroform and ether (ACE) pumped from the ante-room in a long pipe connected to a brass tube tied in the dog's trachea. The tube 'came under the floor between the two rooms and was brought up through the table,' which explained why the accusers could neither see, hear, nor smell the anaesthetic and tubing. The dog remained unconscious throughout the operation.

There was much contradictory evidence from various medical witnesses about the efficacy of various doses of morphine and ACE, including a diversionary account from Francis Gotch, professor of physiology at Oxford University, of how he had recently been called upon to anaesthetise a celebrated greyhound called Fullerton, a one time winner of the Waterloo Cup who had to have his eye removed. Alf Sewell, a prominent vet, told the court he believed Bayliss's system would be highly unlikely to give satisfactory results and that an anaesthetist would always be necessary. But big names on the other side, including Frederick Hobday, professor of the Royal Veterinary College, said they felt Bayliss had done all that was necessary.

On the other hand the vivisectors also claimed that Bayliss had actually given the dog too much anaesthesia, which accounted for the animal's failure to respond to the electrodes. With such an overdose the dog may well have died but for a leakage in the tube supplying the anaesthetic, they said. As the lecture room was large and well ventilated it was unlikely that anyone would have smelled such small amounts of ACE – an argument disputed by defence witnesses.

With such conflicting evidence the case eventually boiled down to which side of the argument the jury believed most, and as the libel laws put the onus on Coleridge to prove his accusations rather than on Bayliss to disprove them, the trial swung decisively in the latter's favour.

This Coleridge all-but conceded under cross examination by stating that 'where Dr Bayliss's statement traverses the statement of the two ladies on any question of fact, I have believed the two ladies'. For the most part the two sides merely contradicted each other on the main arguments, yet the prosecution scored the most important victory of the case by forcing Coleridge to admit he had made no attempt to carry out an independent check of the Swedish women's statements, that he had not tackled Bayliss about the incident prior to his St James's Hall speech, that his office had thrown away the original copy of the Swedish student's account, and that he had made some minor alterations and additions to the women's statement before presenting it to the NAVS meeting.

These admissions – along with Coleridge's failure to back up the women's allegations with any corroborating evidence — counted heavily against him. An accomplished performance on the prosecution side by Rufus Isaacs, who, according to one anti-vivisectionist observer 'towered far above the other legal luminaries in the force of his language, the pointedness of his satire, and his scorn of the sentimental' did not help matters either. Isaacs did not hold back when it came to undermining the defence's two key witnesses, and he was accused of 'skilfully playing upon the chords of sex and race prejudice' by questioning the Swedish women's right to criticise British scientists. With typical but effective overstatement, he used his opening address to paint Lind-af-Hageby as 'the most ignorant person that ever entered a lecture room for medical students'.

In a generally even-handed summing up, apart from one jaundiced reference to the *Shambles of Science* as a 'hysterical' book, Lord Alverstone stressed to the jury that although they had heard 'a very important case' of national interest they should not be swayed by general arguments on the moral validity of vivisection – even though such matters had naturally come up during the trial.

It took the jury just 25 minutes to come to their unanimous

decision: Bayliss won his libel action and Coleridge, to loud applause from the medical contingent in the public gallery, was fined heavy damages of £2,000 plus £3,000 costs. In today's prices that would amount to something like £250,000 in total.

Six days later, on 24 November 1903, Bayliss announced that he had donated the money to University College for the furtherance and promotion of physiological research, although he didn't take up a provocative suggestion in the Daily Mail that his legacy be christened The Stephen Coleridge Vivisection Fund. The money, as Bayliss's son Leonard noted with ironic relish many years later, 'continues to be available ... in any way that the professor of physiology may wish – including at times the purchase of dogs for experimental purposes'.

Several years after the trial, Coleridge claimed in the anti-vivisectionist Zoopholist magazine that Bayliss could hardly wait to get his money. 'The verdict was given at six o'clock in the evening and at half past ten the next morning Mr Bayliss's solicitor sent round for the £2,000,' he wrote. 'I suppose he thought that was a way of manifesting the distinguished and dignified manners of the high physiological circles. He received my cheque for the amount before luncheon, which I may be permitted to surmise caused him a sense of deflation.'

Coleridge did not have to wait long for reimbursement, for national coverage of the brown dog trial had temporarily swelled the coffers of the anti-vivisection movement. The Daily News opened a special brown dog subscription fund which within four months had attracted public donations of more than £5,700, covering the costs and damages of £5,000 plus a little extra for general NAVS funds.

Coleridge boasted that the whole exercise had cost his organisation 'not a farthing' and there is little doubt that despite his defeat in the High Court the free publicity was valuable beyond measure to an anti-vivisection movement which, at the time, had been in organised existence for barely 25 years. National, regional and even foreign newspapers devoted hundreds of column inches to the case and, by extension, the moral debate on vivisection. John Vyvyan, in his 1971 book *The Dark face of science*, claimed the trial was 'the best piece of publicity the NAVS has ever had' and Coleridge himself later acknowledged that it 'roused the public to the support of the anti-vivisection cause as nothing else before or since has done'.

The Daily News led the crusade, attacking the jury's decision as a miscarriage of justice and calling on its readers to consider boycotting charity funds set up by hospitals practising vivisection. 'We can only say

the trial

Court room characters as portrayed by the Daily Graphic

that the whole admitted details of the operation – the laughter of the students, the throwing down of the unhappy animal after the operation, the careless indifference of all concerned – throw no favourable light on the state of mind and morals produced by scientific study under modern conditions,' it said on the day after the verdict. 'This is not a matter which can be allowed to rest here. We are all responsible for this hideous defiance of the laws of humanity.'

Although the Daily News was backed by other dailies such as The Star and The Sun, overall press reaction to Coleridge's defence was generally less favourable. Journalistic commentators on both sides of the debate thought the damages heavy and excessive, and were quick to censure the rowdyism of some medical students in the public gallery, whom The Times accused of 'medical hooliganism.' But conservative papers were staunchly supportive of the medical establishment and even the more liberal organs, though sympathising with the plight of the dog, continued to argue the case for vivisection. The Observer, for instance, reluctantly came out in favour of animal experiments as 'a terrible necessity of science', warning Coleridge and his supporters that they 'must be careful not to make false and reckless charges which themselves are no less acts of cruelty, though not to the brute creation'.

The Observer was not the only newspaper or magazine to suggest that Coleridge's personal reputation had been damaged by the trial. A leader in The Times on 19 November 1903 claimed that 'the defendant, when placed in the witness box, did as much damage to his own case as the time at his disposal would allow,' and even the Zoophilist conceded that Coleridge had paid the price for forsaking the 'cautious habit of his predecessors,' who had traditionally made accusations based on records of animal experiments collected by the vivisectors themselves. 'The testimony of the two lady witnesses, though no doubt witnesses of truth, was not sufficient to sustain the charge made by Mr Coleridge. Anti-vivisectionists may be grieved but can hardly be surprised that a verdict was given for Dr Bayliss,' it said. The Baptist Times denounced vivisection as 'wicked and diabolical,' yet regretted 'that Mr Coleridge should have rested so serious a charge upon the doubtful statements made by two Swedish ladies' – and the Birmingham Post wondered how he could have been 'so devoid of common sense' as to believe their story without corroboration.

The British Medical Journal argued – a trifle too dramatically – that the NAVS's 'dark and crooked ways' had been 'laid bare by the searchlight of the High Court', and that 'their most aggressive champion stands before the world crestfallen and clothed with shame'. Coleridge, it said, 'typifies the fanaticism which prefers that human beings should suffer rather than that animals should be inconvenienced, with its insane hatred of biological research, its readiness to believe all evil of those who cultivate that branch of science, and its unscrupulousness in the choice of weapons in warfare against them'.

Words like that from the medical profession would have mattered little to Coleridge, but the widespread criticism from other quarters of his performance in court would have hurt – particularly as he was a barrister. On the other hand Coleridge must surely have known he had little chance of winning the case, and would probably have built some measure of public humiliation into his calculations when he made the speech at St James's Hall.

There is little doubt that he deliberately engineered the brown dog trial; in court he admitted he had asked Lind-af-Hageby and Schartau if they would be prepared to stand up and repeat their claims on oath because he expected a subsequent action for libel and slander. He knew directly after he had made his speech, he told the court, that proceedings were going to be instituted, and he had tipped off the Daily News to get maximum publicity.

In the long term, though, the damage to Coleridge's reputation appears to have been minimal. The libel case certainly exposed the negative side to his passion, which was a tendency to allow his combative instincts and pig-headedness to gain the upper hand, but the trial also brought him more fame than he had known before. A lover of life with connections at the highest levels of British society, a great controversialist and a long-term friend of Oscar Wilde, he was hardly a man to be shaken off the trail of anything he believed in, and would never have considered abandoning his public role in the anti-vivisectionist cause – which he believed, through his family roots, was a 'consecrated inheritance'. On balance he made a sound decision to generate publicity through a trial, even if at some short-term cost to his credibility. He lost, but the trial made animal experiments a topic of public debate for several precious months.

It also, for a while at least, united an increasingly divided anti-vivisectionist movement. The NAVS had prospered as the largest anti-vivisection organisation since its foundation as the Victoria Street Society in 1875, and was largely responsible for the lobbying that led to the creation of the Cruelty to Animals Act, which stayed in force for more than 100 years. But by 1898, a year after Coleridge had become its honorary secretary at the age of 43, a damaging internal argument had developed over whether the society should settle for more gradual change via progressively stronger legislation or push only for outright abolition of animal experiments.

Although Coleridge accepted the gradualist approach, Frances Cobbe, the ageing yet still fiercely determined woman who had been the society's co-founder and guiding light before Coleridge's arrival, would accept no tinkering, only abolition. Neither side would yield, and after a stormy executive meeting had voted to adopt the gradualist route in February 1898 Cobbe, aged 76, broke away in May to form the British Union for the Abolition of Vivisection (BUAV).

During and immediately after the brown dog trial, however, the two sides came together in a rare public show of unity against the University College – and a meeting of the BUAV central managers committee on the day after the trial even passed a sympathetic resolution 'to express its sincere regret at the issue of the Coleridge v Bayliss libel case and to cordially sympathise with Mr Coleridge'. The abolitionist *Zoophilist* couldn't resist the opportunity to hope that Coleridge would now 'see the fallacy of the policy of half measures which he [has] imposed on his society ... and to recognise that nothing short of the absolute prohibition of all vivisection will put any check upon this yearly increasing and ever more cruel ... practice.' But the trial did usher in a brief and significant thaw in an otherwise icy relationship.

For the Swedish women and their 200-page book, the trial was a watershed too. After the jury had delivered its verdict, the Covent Garden publisher Ernest Bell, an anti-vivisectionist sympathiser who had brought out *Shambles of Science* in July 1903, gave an undertaking to withdraw the book from circulation, promising not to promote or publish it again and handing over all unsold copies to Bayliss's solicitors (much to the annoyance of Lind-af-Hageby and Schartau, who had made sure that the names of lecturers and demonstrators had been left out).

But a month later a BUAV meeting was already considering 'the question of re-publishing *Shambles of Science* under another title and with the chapter entitled *Fun* eliminated'. The sanitised reprint, which included a new first chapter called *The Vivisections of the Brown Dog*, sold heavily. By 1913, thanks to 'continuous demand', it had already run to five editions, though nowadays only a few copies remain.

Although *Shambles of Science* was written jointly by Lind-af-Hageby and Schartau, it was Lind-af-Hageby who stole the limelight. Schartau, a language expert and part-time poet, was less combative than her companion and found public speaking difficult, as she showed at the High Court. Lind-af-Hageby swiftly became a sought-after personality in London society, much in demand as a speaker and willing to lend her name to various causes, including the battle for women's rights. She also continued her efforts to stir the brown dog controversy – even after the court defeat, which the medical profession had hoped would draw a line under the affair. Lind-af-Hageby was to play as big a part as anyone in the brown dog's posthumous career.

the fountain

genesis of the memorial ... search for a sponsor ... finding a home in radical Battersea ... conservative opposition ... putting it to the vote

THERE WAS LITTLE time to digest the libel trial result, for within a few days Lind-af-Hageby found herself approached by a woman who had hatched a plan to keep the brown dog case on the boil.

Her name was Louisa Woodward, an accomplished linguist, speaker, and organiser, who was honorary secretary of the Society for United Prayer for the Prevention of Cruelty to Animals and of the International Anti-Vivisection Council. Woodward, a well-to-do woman who lived in north Kensington, had fixed on the idea of creating a permanent memorial to the brown dog in the form of a drinking fountain. Such fountains were popular at the time, and local authorities would often accept them as gifts for use by the general public in open spaces or parks. Woodward believed she could find a sympathetic London council to take her memorial and keep the brown dog controversy ticking along. She met Lind-af-Hageby, who approved, and the plan was set in motion.

Using money raised by public subscription (and possibly some cash from her own sources), Woodward decided to commission, at a cost of £120, a bronze representation of the brown dog from the sculptor Joseph Whitehead, whose company in Harleyford Road near London's Kennington Oval specialised mainly in church-related items such as pulpits but had also designed a number of drinking fountains and cattle troughs – and eventually went on to produce the Titanic Memorial in Southampton.

On the granite base a fountain would provide water for people and dogs alike, and on the pillar there would be a powerful and deliberately controversial inscription, bearing the hallmarks of Woodward's writing style, which read: 'In memory of the brown terrier dog done to death in the laboratories of University College in February 1903, after having endured vivisection extending over more than two months and having been handed over from one vivisector to another till death came to his release. Also in memory of the 232 dogs vivisected at the same place during the year 1902. Men and women of England, how long shall these things be?'

the fountain

With the help of Captain William Simpson, secretary of the Metropolitan Drinking Fountain and Cattle Trough Association, Woodward had first approached the London County Council for permission to erect the memorial either at Golders Hill Park in north London or Battersea Park in the south of the capital. After three months deliberation the LCC turned down the offer in early May 1904 on the basis that the fountain was 'undesirable'. She turned instead to Hendon council in north London, which said it would be happy to place the fountain at an alternative site in Hendon Public Park. But when Woodward visited the park she began to feel Hendon was far too quiet, and that few people would actually walk past what she intended to be a high-profile monument. So she turned her attentions back to Battersea, writing to the local council on 8 June 1904 to seek permission 'to erect a granite drinking fountain with a trough for dogs at the base on the top of Lavender Hill', near Battersea Town Hall, 'or in such other place as the borough may deem suitable'.

A year earlier, in April 1903, Battersea had turned down the offer of a fountain and dog trough from the Metropolitan Drinking Fountain and Cattle Trough Association, claiming there was 'no available site'. This time the council looked as if it would respond more favourably. The memorial was not destined to be accepted without a fight, yet clearly Woodward and her friends had a chosen a sympathetic recipient. In fact there could have been no more logical place for her to go than Battersea.

On a purely personal level, Woodward had connections with the borough through the royal chaplain and anti-vivisectionist Erskine Clarke, vicar of Battersea, as well as Lady Constance Battersea, who was a vice president of the BUAV. In more general terms Battersea was the most natural place for her to find a home for the memorial. By 1904 the area had acquired a national reputation as a hotbed of alternative politics and a breeding ground for trade unionism, republicanism, anti-colonialism, municipal socialism, Irish home rulers, suffragettes – and anti-vivisectionists. There would have been few places in the country where the brown dog could have expected a more sympathetic reception.

In the first half of the 19th century Battersea had been an essentially rural market gardening area of no more than 6,000 souls, a south London backwater famous only for its fertile alluvial soil and its locally grown sticks of asparagus, sold in what were universally known as 'Battersea bundles'.

By the late 1800s it had been transformed into a filthy, densely populated industrial stretch of riverfront, heaving with more than 100,000 people – most living in cramped, jerry-built slums cheek by jowl with their places of work – flour mills, iron works, laundries, barge builders, gas works, paint and candle factories, engineering and chemical works and the railway, which had sparked off the fierce pace of industrialisation when it spawned the massive complex of lines at Clapham Junction on its way to Waterloo. It was said that you could smell Battersea before you saw it.

In the ten years between the censuses of 1861 and 1871, the population of this impoverished Thameside area between the bridges at Vauxhall and Wandsworth had more than doubled from 19,600 to 54,016 and by 1881 had tipped 107,000. By the time Woodward came forward with her statue it had risen to around 165,000.

Battersea had become a place to avoid if you could possibly help it; a dark, soot-laden contrast to the good living of Chelsea on the opposite bank of the Thames, a crowded enclave of poor pay, unemployment, undernourishment, disease and shortened lifespans.

Battersea-born Harry Wicks, in his book *Keeping My Head*, remembered a hard life which tested the self-reliance and resourcefulness of every resident: 'We never suffered the stark, brutal, unrelieved poverty of the East End ... but in north Battersea, huddled against the evil smelling factories, lived workers' families that occupied one room only, in streets of tenement houses. The difference between the East End worker and those in Battersea was marginal.'

The fight for survival bred a close-knit community, which for the most part kept itself to itself; Battersea folk were an insular lot. 'No major roads out of London passed our way and the secondary ones merely included us *en route* to somewhere else, raising scarcely a ripple in the flow of our everyday life,' remembered Edward Ezard in his autobiography, *Battersea Boy*. 'We found content with others of our own kind, a tribe within a tribe ... sharing common values and standards.'

There was another side to Battersea's insularity. As the locals looked to each other for support, so they also began to develop a sense of solidarity, fostered and fuelled by the battles for workplace rights at their local factories and railway yards. The Battersea of 1904 had already become what Wicks and others later recognised as 'a cradle of working class politics.'

Battersea's fiery reputation was initially borne of its trade unionist activity and was personified by John Burns, a locally born engineer who began work at the age of ten at Price's Candles factory on the Battersea riverfront. An accomplished orator, teetotaller, republican and non-

the fountain

The colossus of Battersea: John Burns as seen by Punch magazine

smoker who, according to one contemporary account, 'never wears an overcoat no matter how bitter the weather may be', Burns was known widely in London as 'the man with the red flag', and came to national prominence as a leader of the London dock strike in 1889, the same year he was elected as Battersea's representative to the London County Council.

Three years later in 1892 he became one of the first three Labour

MPs to enter Parliament – along with Keir Hardie at South-West Ham and Havelock Wilson at Middlesbrough – when the Battersea electorate returned him as their Independent Labour MP. Although he later blotted his socialist copy book by joining Sir Henry Campbell Bannerman's Liberal cabinet in 1905 (becoming the first working class man to reach cabinet level), Burns was a talismanic figure for many in the borough, a symbol to the outside world of Battersea's radical leanings. In the 1920s, its electorate went on to elect an Indian-born Communist MP, Shapurji Saklatvala.

Battersea was also home to the anti-slavery and anti-vivisectionist campaigner William Wilberforce as well as Charlotte Despard, a formidable, rebellious Irish socialist who helped the destitute in Nine Elms by dishing out cheap food, setting up clinics and running mothers' meetings. Like Burns, Despard was a keen advocate of temperance, but she was also an anti-vivisectionist vegetarian and supported any number of radical groups and campaigns, including home rule for Ireland. She came to national prominence chiefly as a determined and highly active champion of women's suffrage, a cause which, as 'the mother of Battersea', she did much to link with the borough's name.

Battersea's progressive outlook was, however, associated more with its left-wing local council than prominent figures like Burns and Despard. Battersea Borough Council, even to the grudging acknowledgment of the politically unsympathetic South Western Star newspaper, was 'rightly regarded as an awesome body' throughout the country. Any Battersea resident travelling to another part of Britain could usually expect a barrage of questions about the council's latest doings, which generated glee and outrage in equal measure, depending on political outlook. Conservative newspapers nurtured a morbid fascination with the activities of a council run by ordinary working men, and The Times of 18 September 1902 felt moved to devote a whole page to a denunciation of Battersea's policies, describing the borough as a 'municipal mecca' that carried out its business 'in strict accord with the most advanced type of municipal socialism'.

Relentlessly criticised by the opposition Municipal Reform Party for its high spending on public services and a willingness to let the rates take the strain, Battersea's Progressive Alliance of Labourite and Liberal councillors took a radical stand on most of the burning issues of the day, despite the sometimes delicate state of its coalition. Based around the Battersea Trades and Labour Council, which held together a disparate confederation of different liberal organisations, the Battersea Labour

League, various trade union branches and the Battersea branch of the marxist-leaning Social Democratic Federation, it proved remarkably resilient in the face of nationwide disapproval.

The borough's large Irish population guaranteed support within the council for home rule and by extension anti-colonialism, prompting the progressives to give their backing to a number of independence movements. They were heavily involved in the campaign to stop the war against the Boers, who they saw as anti-imperialists fighting British colonialism and in February 1903, amid general consternation, pointedly refused to help a national government appeal for funds to establish a hospital for sick soldiers who fought in the Boer War. Four years later they refused to fly the union flag across the borough on Empire Day.

The strong republicanism of many progressive councillors had also stunned the nation when in 1902 councillors refused – with the support of Burns – to seal a loyal address to Edward VII on his coronation. Had the council existed in the 1980s it would certainly have attracted a 'loony left' tag from its detractors. In 1904 the progressives had widespread working class support and a safe majority, which encouraged them to roam across all kinds of political issues, not just on a narrow home front but also across international boundaries.

It was on domestic matters, though, that the progressives were better able to combine rhetoric with practicality. Since the creation of an innovative direct works department just before the turn of the century, the progressive administration had been able to demonstrate its commitment to improving the health and welfare of its citizens by building swimming baths, a disinfecting station for de-lousing the poor, a mortuary, its own generating station to supply cheap electricity for street lights and homes, and a sterilising unit to provide safe milk for local babies.

Many progressive councillors were vehemently opposed to compulsory vaccination, not just because there was cruelty involved in making the vaccines but because they believed it was a suppression of the freedom of choice. One of their number, William Watts, even appeared in court charged with refusing to allow his son Lionel to have a jab. The case was dismissed on a technicality, although the publicity it brought helped councillors in their encouragement of Battersea mothers to boycott the large-scale vaccination programme brought in by the Vaccination Act of 1898. The party as a whole believed in preventing disease through better hygiene and improved standards of living, and thanks to its public works programme could claim some success in that direction. The infant mortality rate for Battersea fell from 159 per thousand in 1900 to 131 per

Battersea Town Hall: a mecca of municipal socialism

thousand in 1905, and the number of typhoid cases dropped over the same period from 205 a year to 27.

The council also subsidised free public concerts for the poor and opened a gym for local boys, but pride of place went to its 'homes for the working class' built by the direct works department and opened by Burns in August 1903. A superior mix of three- and four-roomed tenements plus a selection of five-roomed houses on six acres of land off Latchmere Road near Battersea Park, the Latchmere Estate was the first council housing to be built by the borough and one of the earliest municipal estates in the United Kingdom.

The 315 working class families who moved in there were given the unusual privileges of electric lighting, large rooms, the latest in cooking and heating equipment, a garden to each house, and their own front door – all for 11s 6d a week. They were simple yet attractive houses, which are still in demand to this day and are now protected in a conservation area. Built next to the Latchmere swimming baths – also one of the first municipal amenities of its kind – they rejoiced in appropriately optimistic street names such as Reform Street, Freedom Street and, more controversially, Joubert Street, after a Boer general. There was also a Burns Road, and the estate was the local MP's pride and joy. Burns was a 'gas and water socialist' who, despite his later liberal leanings, was a consistent and long-term supporter of municipal socialism. At the opening ceremony he put forward a vision of Latchmere's 'happy, healthy homes for sober and industrious workmen' which would not be tainted with an off licence 'or degraded by a beer house'.

Temperance was also a strong force on the nearby Shaftesbury Estate, an immense network of 1,135 cottages built on behalf of the strongly anti-vivisectionist Lord Shaftesbury between 1872 and 1875 by the Artisans, Labourers and General Dwellings Company, whose objective was 'to help the working classes ... raise their position in the social scale'.

Outside of the council's innovative sphere, the people of Battersea had also contrived to provide a sympathetic environment for a number of alternative, experimental institutions. There was the pioneering 'people's university' of Battersea Polytechnic, founded in 1894 to give 'young men and women belonging to the poorer classes' the chance to progress to university or to learn a trade. There was the famous and innovative Battersea Dogs' Home, which had moved early in its life to the borough to rescue stray dogs from the perils of vivisection. And, significantly from Woodward's point of view, there was the elegantly designed Anti-Vivisection Hospital overlooking Battersea Park.

Opened in 1902 as the Battersea General on the corner of Prince of Wales Drive and Albert Bridge Road, the 'Anti Vivi', as it was affectionately known by the locals, refused to take part in any animal experiments,

The loony left: how The Sketch saw Battersea's progressive councillors

would have no vivisectors on its staff, offered homeopathic medicine and pledged never to use vivisection should it develop a medical school. As a consequence the Lancet and BMJ refused to take its job adverts, but it was a popular hospital nonetheless. In 1903, the year of the brown dog trial, it treated 82 inpatients and 13,118 outpatients, but by 1906 medical staff were seeing 245 inpatients, 20,010 outpatients and were carrying out 359 operations.

The only general hospital for men, women and children in Battersea, it ministered to a wide catchment area and soon drew Lind-af-Hageby on to its board of management. It remained an integral part of Battersea life until it was closed in 1971 and was replaced, some time later, by a sheltered housing complex.

Battersea's hospital, its dogs' home and its radical local authority were clearly attractive rallying points for Woodward and Lind-af-Hageby. They knew that few areas of London would have even considered the idea of accepting their memorial, let alone taking it to full council for a vote of approval. In Battersea they had a better than even chance.

Certainly the council's initial reaction was encouragingly swift. It took only three days for Woodward's proposal to reach the agenda of the borough's highways and dustings committee, which debated the idea on 30 May 1904. Members on the committee recommended that the council should accept Woodward's offer with alacrity and thanks, with the proviso that it should 'report later as to a site for the fountain'.

A fortnight later the same committee adjourned again without having decided on a favoured site, but by its meeting on 4 July 1904 there was movement. The borough surveyor read out the inscription and reported that the fountain could be fixed in Falcon Road at the northern end of Lavender Hill, just a few yards from Clapham Junction railway station. Both the inscription and the Falcon Road site were approved with only one dissenter.

The Falcon Road location didn't please the full council, however, and by 18 July 1904 the highways and dustings committee members were reconsidering their original plan. They boiled the possible sites down to six: on the Prince of Wales Drive near the Anti-Vivisection Hospital, on Battersea Bridge Road in front of the congregational church, on Battersea Rise at the junction of Lavender Sweep, on Battersea Square in Battersea village, on Bridge Road West in front of Lammas Hall, or on a planned new recreation ground on the Latchmere Estate.

In a show of hands four of the options failed to attract a single vote, and there were just two in favour of the site in front of the congregational

the fountain

church. The winner, with four supporters, was the Latchmere Recreation Ground. Two weeks later the full council gave its stamp of approval.

By this stage it was the inscription, not the position of the fountain, that was causing problems. The first controversy over the words on the memorial's pillar had surfaced during the full council meeting of 13 July 1904, when Municipal Reform councillor Peter Haythornthwaite had moved that the inscription should be amended. He was defeated by 25 votes to 11, but his party raised the issue again two weeks later, losing by a bigger margin of 31 to 10.

The plans for the fountain had by now come to the attention of the University College hierarchy, who agreed at their council meeting on 25 July 1904 to send an urgent letter to the Battersea town clerk. 'The college and its professors cannot believe that your council will associate themselves with a libel to this nature,' it thundered. 'They hope to hear from you with an assurance that no site will be granted. If such an inscription were really in contemplation with the approval of your council, proceedings would have to be taken to protect the work of the college and the reputation of those engaged upon it.'

The letter met with studied silence; although the municipal reformers tried twice in the succeeding month to force the mayor into taking legal advice, the progressives were in bullish mood and would have nothing to do with the university's threats. They refused even to furnish the college with details of their decisions about the fountain, although opposition councillors appeared to be in regular contact with Bayliss's supporters and were only too willing to fill in the gaps.

As 1904 turned into 1905, the university elders could only gnash their teeth as the council's direct works department got to work laying out the Latchmere Recreation Ground, where the memorial would stand. Partly asphalted and bordered by flower beds, the recreation ground was the icing on the cake of the Latchmere Estate, a rectangular-shaped acre of land on Burns Road that would allow children to play and tenants to stroll. The fountain would have pride of place, dead centre on the path where locals would cut across the grounds to reach Battersea Park Road.

Progress on the recreation ground was painfully slow, however – partly due to cash-flow problems with the Central (Unemployed) Body for London, which was supposed to be paying for local unemployed people to work on the site. There were long periods when no work was carried out at all, and as the days dragged along, Woodward became increasingly agitated at the delay. The memorial had been ready and paid for since early December 1904, yet she began to despair that it would ever see the light of day. Several letters were dispatched to the council during 1905, asking when an unveiling date might be set, but they were met with vague replies that work still had some way to go. In the end Woodward became so frustrated that she asked the council to find somewhere else to put the fountain, although she was told Latchmere was the only available site. Eventually, after more pressing inquiries in July 1906, the highways and dustings committee felt able to recommend that the ground was 'sufficiently laid out to allow the erection of the fountain' and that the memorial should be in place by September that year.

By that stage University College council members appear to have realised that the memorial would become a reality whether they liked it or not – and fearful that they had no real grounds for suing, they decided to ask their solicitors 'if they think it desirable to take further counsel's opinion for the purpose of advising the college as to what action, if any, should be taken'. Many Battersea councillors felt the college's libel threat was mere bluff, and in private the university hierarchy clearly felt less bullish than it did in public.

Although the highways and dustings committee had given a swift and positive reply to the International Anti-Vivisection Council's letter inquiring about progress at Latchmere, the final niceties took much longer

Battersea General Hospital, otherwise known as 'the Anti-Vivi'

when it came to full council at Battersea Town Hall nine days later on 11 July. In what the Wandsworth Borough News described as 'lively scenes' and the South Western Star as 'great heat and excitement', the municipal reformers made a desperate last ditch effort to throw out the memorial. 'At times everybody shouted at once, and the contagion spread to the gallery, where excited people got up and leaned over the front at the risk of breaking their necks,' said the South Western Star.

Tempers were frayed even further when progressive members spotted an uninvited 'stranger' named Mr Dobell trying to keep his head down at the press table. Under questioning Mr Dobell admitted he was not a member of the press – and that he was in fact a shorthand writer sent clandestinely by the University College. After heated debate and confessions from two municipal reformers that they had encouraged the man to be there, a vote was carried to expel him from the meeting. The wrangle over Mr Dobell was 'short and fiery'; the rest of the meeting developed into 'intense acrimony'.

A few of the progressives had begun to waver, and it was one of their number, the vegetarian alderman George Smith, who moved that the memorial should be put on ice. He backed the municipal reform view that the statue was potentially libellous and would open up old wounds, although he gave his speech, said the South Western Star, 'like a man who is performing a painful duty in obedience to the dictates of his conscience'.

There were various votes on various amendments, but in the end the progressives won through by 26 to 19 votes on a show of hands. When the ruling party forced a division so that the voting pattern of the waverers would be officially recorded, the majority rose to 32 for and 21 against.

The key to the progressives' victory on the night – aside from the fact that they had an in-built majority – was the production of an International Anti-Vivisection Council document that pledged to indemnify the council against any costs and fines that might arise out of a court case against the memorial's inscription. As a gesture of goodwill a £300 cheque had already been signed in the council's name and deposited in the bank on 22 August as a guarantee. The anti-vivisectionists urged the council not to be timid and to go ahead with its plans.

Most progressive councillors needed little encouragement, for they believed that having approved of the inscription more than a year ago they could not disgrace themselves by drawing back at the last minute. Councillor Augustus West revealed that there had been veiled threats that 'a number of students would come down to Battersea and destroy the fountain' if it was ever erected, but he urged his colleagues not to be

An aerial view of the Latchmere Estate, immediately above the railway. The recreation ground is just visible top right

frightened by such taunts. Councillor James Brown promised that any medical students straying into Battersea would be met by 'something more than passive resisters' and argued that a libel action against the inscription would 'throw a great light' on the way hospitals were run. The waverers should keep faith with the anti-vivisectors because Battersea could 'stand the racket' of any subsequent controversy, he said.

Not all of the waverers were yet convinced but the deed was now done and the unveiling ceremony for the memorial was set for 15 September 1906. There was one last chance for the conservatives to put a spoke in the wheel when councillors met again to authorise the sealing of the deed of indemnity. But although there was concerted opposition from councillor John Astill, who said the deed was not worth the paper it was written on, it was signed nonetheless, and now it was too late to turn back anyway: the opening ceremony was ready for the following Saturday. A municipal reformer tried to raise one last point as the meeting drew to a close, but his fellow councillors 'yapped like so many brown dogs' and drowned him out. The mayor ended the meeting without any further speeches.

By now the memorial had caught the local public's imagination; it had become a source of fierce debate across the borough. No-one really disagreed that a fountain would be worth having, but whether it should involve a brown dog was another matter. The division, predictably, fell roughly along political lines.

The South London Press favoured a plain fountain, undedicated to anyone, human or animal. 'The recent spell of hot and dusty weather has brought to the notice of many the dearth of drinking water fountains throughout the boroughs of Wandsworth and Battersea, and a movement on the part of the respective borough councils to remedy the matter would earn the appreciation of many,' it said on 8 September 1906. More fountains, it contended, would also encourage Battersea folk to quench their first with pure water rather than 'seek relief in the nearest public house'.

Ironically in the light of subsequent events it argued that 'if objection is raised that such fountains are abused by children and destructive boys, well, we have our police, who would not object to the small task of keeping an eye on them'. But it did not approve of a brown dog, or a potentially libellous inscription.

The South Western Star was more equivocal, but hopeful that the whole escapade would eventually backfire on the radicals. 'We shall see what we see on Saturday when the little brown dog is to be unveiled,' it said on the eve of the opening. 'The council is already indemnified against all risk, but unanimity does not exist even among the progressives as to the enterprise to which the council has committed itself. Nor is there hopefulness. "It will be a serious thing for us" we heard a member of the progressives say dolefully on Wednesday evening. But there is still some hope – hope that a lawsuit at the proper time might stimulate the burgesses to vote as they have never voted, and that the happy result will be a council composed in the main of municipal reformers.'

unveiled

a nervous opening ceremony ... a phoney war ... an attack on a foggy night ... punishment for the offenders ... national prominence for the dog once again

EXCEPT FOR THE overcast weather, the official unveiling of the brown dog memorial on 15 September 1906 ran more smoothly than its supporters could have hoped.

There were no protests from Battersea residents, as the local papers had hoped, nor was there any show of defiance from the students across the river, who had threatened to disrupt the proceedings. Just an interested throng of people from the Latchmere Estate and a collection of the great and good from the anti-vivisectionist movement.

Charlotte Despard was there, plus the Countess of Seafield, the Reverend Conrad Noel, Louisa Woodward, and, according to one account, George Bernard Shaw. They sat on a platform specially erected for the speakers, while a semi-circle of women and children nestled around the covered fountain. 'The feminine element included several determined looking ladies in felt hats and short skirts,' said the Wandsworth Borough News, in a veiled reference to the suffragettes who had already tied their colours to the dog's tail.

At 3.30pm the progressive trade unionist tailor Bill Rines, mayor of Battersea, stood to open the proceedings. The rain came down heavily and a smattering of umbrellas opened. The council, he said, had been threatened with 'all sorts of pains and penalties' but was prepared to take the consequences of its actions and had adopted the monument 'in the interests of humanity and of the animal world'. To murmurs of approval he criticised the 'waywardness of medical science' that had produced doctors who were often immune to the sufferings of animals and even their own patients. It was not just the doctors, he said; there were men who made noises against vivisection yet hunted animals in their leisure time, and women 'who clothe themselves in the skin of the seal or delight themselves in wearing plumage which has been torn from living birds'.

Joseph Jeffery, a London county councillor and former mayor of Chelsea, stood to formally hand over the statue to the mayor on behalf of the International Anti-Vivisection Council, praising the local authority for its bravery. Rines pulled a string and the cloth fell to the ground to reveal a polished red granite base 7ft 6in in height, with the 18in tall bronze dog sitting proudly on top. Halfway down was a drinking fountain for humans; at the bottom a small trough for dogs.

The dog, like its real life model, looked more mongrel than terrier, but it was alert, friendly, wide-eyed, innocent and surprisingly dignified, the epitome of man's best friend. Some of its opponents later criticised the sculpture's artistic merits, although for the most part it was well received. To Edward Ford, who wrote a pamphlet about the dog two years later, it had 'a pleasing appearance' with 'a mild countenance and sleek head which bore no trace of the martyr's crown with which his fame had been invested'. The Morning Leader praised its 'handsome, wistful' face. 'No memorial in London has the unique interest which surrounds that of the brown dog,' it added.

Yet the critical acclaim was largely irrelevant, as the memorial's charm lay more in the fact that it had been sculpted not as a work of art but as a utilitarian tribute to a cause. It was a fountain, not a statue; plain and unfussy, like the working class homes which surrounded it. And it was something for the local people to adopt as their own. Tenants on the Latchmere Estate would use the footpath on which the memorial was laid for easy access to Battersea Park Road and would pass it almost every day, stopping to take a drink if necessary. Children playing in the area would run there to quench their thirst.

As the mayor unveiled the monument, local kids sang *Ring the Bells of Mercy* through the lashing rain and Councillor William West drew the first cupful of water from the fountain. There was palpable relief that the ceremony had passed off without incident, as there had been an atmosphere of suppressed tension all afternoon.

'Half-expectant, half-defiant glances were cast in the direction of the entrance gates, for rumours had been going round that hospital students would show their displeasure with the whole affair in their own peculiar way,' said the Wandsworth Borough News. 'The prospect cast its shadow over the gathering unmistakably, and the friends of the brown dog did not breathe quite freely until the last word had been spoken.' The student threats had been taken seriously enough for the council to fit the dog with an electric bell connected to a watchman's hut, so that any attempt to tamper with the fountain could be detected early. 'No-one could give the dog a friendly stroke without causing bells to ring,' said one reporter.

As the crowd of well-wishers dispersed, representatives of the local and national press went home to write down their reactions. Fuelled by a journalistic relish of the sense of impending doom, they mostly chose to

The monument showing the drinking fountain halfway up and trough at the base

damn the dog and its naive adoptive owners. 'Of course no reasonable objection could be offered to the setting up of a structure which served to inculcate the duty of kindness,' said the South Western Star of the following Friday. 'But it is another thing to accept a gift which probably would never have been offered if the donors had not desired to give expression to feelings of vindictiveness. The Battersea Borough Council is being used as the instrument of certain persons' ill-will. The gift, with its questionable inscription, could not have been accepted except for the egregious conceit of members of the corporation, who are silly enough to believe they are leading the van of humanitarianism and progress.' It went on to predict that the unveiling would spark off 'a long train of evils' and possible surcharging of councillors.

Through the general condemnation, however, there crept a grudging respect for the council's agenda-setting talents. 'Battersea is controversial even in its monuments,' admitted the London Argus of 22 September 1906. 'In the ordinary way a drinking fountain is one of the most innocent and inoffensive things in the world, but we fear an exception must be made in this case'.

The journalists fully expected to be reporting on the next instalment of the story in a matter of days, and sat back to await developments. 'The deed is done,' said the Wandsworth Borough News. 'It is now up to the hospital authorities to take the next step, if any, in this brown dog affair.' What they got instead was a phoney war lasting more than a year, for hardly anything of interest happened to the dog in the 12 months after it settled down to life on the recreation ground.

Occasionally the locals would spot two or three curious students taking stock of their *bette noire*, perhaps gathering information for some future attack. Usually there was no conflict of any kind, and the outsiders would soon be gone. More often there would be a mistaken cry of 'the students are coming' as an alert local misinterpreted an unusual movement or some unfamiliar faces. Having spent much of 1905 and 1906 arguing about the monument, Battersea councillors couldn't find a single word to say about it for much of 1907, and had no cause to discuss it for months on end.

The phoney war was partly due to the fact that the much-threatened legal action by University College failed to materialise. On Bonfire Night 1906 – just three weeks after the dog was unveiled and only a few days after Battersea's progressives had retained control in the local elections – the college hierarchy received legal advice on the chances of winning a court action for libel. They decided that 'no action be taken in the matter.'

It is hard to tell whether the college administrators ever really believed the inscription on the fountain was libellous, but they must have known they were on stonier ground than when Bayliss took Coleridge to court. Whereas Coleridge had made his statement with at least one eye to provoking a libel action, the backers of the memorial desired no such thing. They wanted the fountain to stand as a permanent challenge to the medical profession – and did not want to risk having it pulled down. Although the inscription was controversial, it was tightly worded compared with Coleridge's 1903 statement. It made no reference to anaesthetics or cruelty, or to violent and purposeful struggles.

Although the vivisectors might not have liked the phraseology of the inscription, the dog had indeed been 'done to death' in the laboratories of University College, and it had incontrovertibly been 'handed over from one vivisector to another' – that much had been admitted in the 1903 court case. Fewer than 232 dogs had been vivisected at the college during the year 1902 – that had been established by a question in Parliament. In fact the only aspect of the inscription that the college could possibly have challenged was its assertion that the dog had 'endured vivisection extending over more than two months', which was a clumsy (or perhaps deliberately sensationalist) way of saying that it had been operated on twice during a period of just over two months.

A barrister could theoretically have argued that such wording was defamatory because it could have been interpreted to mean the dog was being continually operated on 24 hours a day for a period of two months. It is unlikely, though, that any court would have agreed, and the college's legal advisers clearly didn't believe it was a feasible line of attack either. They would probably have reminded college officials that although the 1903 trial was a victory for the vivisectors it was also a publicity coup for the anti-vivisectionists. A second trial would generate more headlines.

So it was that the brown dog remained unmolested for more than a year, free from attacks by the law courts, the pro-vivisectionists, or even the newspapers. Why the students decided to hold themselves at bay is unclear, particularly as the college's decision not to pursue the legal option could have provided an excuse to take the matter onto the streets. Some have argued that the students temporarily lacked a charismatic ringleader to mobilise them, but it may just have been that despite their public high dudgeon, most of them weren't as bothered about the memorial as they professed to be – certainly not enough to go out and break the law.

In the end, the threats of 1906 did eventually become reality. On 20 November 1907, a foggy Wednesday night, a small group of medical students descended on the Latchmere Estate with a crowbar and a sledgehammer, intent on doing some damage. They were led by Howard Lister, a 20-year-old University College undergraduate who had decided that a good London fog would present the ideal opportunity to cross the river and sneak into the dog's territory undetected. He arranged a meeting of interested students in the college's games room that afternoon, and it was put around that anyone who fancied making an assault on the dog should meet at Tottenham Court Road later that afternoon.

At the appointed hour Lister and six friends were at Tottenham Court Road with the hammer and crowbar, but there was no-one else to be seen. They waited in vain for reinforcements but – by now disappointed and slightly anxious – decided to carry through with the plan and board the bus for Battersea.

The fog was slowly beginning to lift when they arrived in Battersea Park Road shortly before 5pm, so they hid themselves behind a conveniently parked furniture van and debated what to do next. Lister took them through to the recreation ground, and as surreptitiously as possible they confronted the dog. 'There it stood before us, this famous lie about which so much had been said and planned,' said Lister in a later account of the evening's activity. 'Some of us who had not been there before had formed quite a different idea of the place in our mind's eye. No wonder therefore that some at first held back and were giving up the idea.'

While the others dithered, one of the keener students, Adolf MacGillicuddy, plucked up the courage to do something. With the crowbar in his hand and the others trying to screen him, he moved up to the fountain and began to wrench at the dog's front legs. The legs were tougher than he had imagined, but were beginning to bend slightly and were showing signs of buckling when a warning shout went up. The students took flight, scattering in different directions.

Lister fled back to Battersea Park Road, but after a short while decided to return quietly to the recreation ground to see if the much-vaunted electric alarm had been working. When he arrived back he saw, to his horror, a crowd of about 25 students talking animatedly in full view of passers by. Most of them were late arrivals who were clearly not as circumspect as the advance party. Before Lister had time to warn them of the risks, 20-year-old Duncan Jones was up at the dog taking 'a mighty blow' with the hammer, and, before he could aim another, was jumped upon by two plain clothes policemen.

There was a half-half hearted shout of 'to the rescue' but most of the students thought better of fighting with the police and ran off into the fog.

Nine of them, including Lister, stayed put, hoping to provide bail for the arrested man as he was dragged off to Lavender Hill police station. Their loyalty proved their undoing, for when they arrived at the station they found themselves arrested too, and thrown into the cells with Jones. 'Which explains,' Lister later wrote, 'how it was that two policeman captured ten medical students, a fact which has set half the London police wondering how they did it'.

The ten were bailed out by a University College staff member and appeared before magistrate Paul Taylor at South Western Police Court in Lavender Hill on the following morning, 21 November 1907. Charged along with Lister, Jones and MacGillicuddy were William Mansfield (22), Arthur Idris (22), Canute Deuntzer (22), Robert Liscombe (19), Burford Norman (18), Julian Taylor (18) and Edward Saunders (22) – all medical students at the University College and Middlesex hospitals. They pleaded guilty to maliciously damaging the monument, a charge brought against them by Battersea council.

The court heard that the authorities had been expecting some action. Renewed threats against the memorial had been made about five weeks previously, perhaps to coincide with the first anniversary of its unveiling, perhaps also due to renewed interest generated by the Metropolitan Hospital Sunday Fund's refusal to award its customary annual grant to the Anti-Vivisection Hospital, a decision which some attributed to disapproval of the nearby fountain. Lister had therefore been right to be cautious, for Scotland Yard had told local police to supplement the watchman by keeping a special look out. Nonetheless the students' foray seems to have been discovered more or less by accident, as the two policemen involved, Sergeant Ellis and PC Daffern, were off duty. They lived on the Latchmere Estate and were alerted by their children who, returning from school, passed a group of young men and overheard them talking about the dog. The children ran home and informed their parents, who then kept a watch by mixing anonymously with the offenders.

As it was, they missed the first attack by MacGillicuddy, although Sergeant Ellis was on hand to see Jones take the hammer from a bag and make a 'ha'penny sized' dent in the memorial. Jones was surprised to see the police and frustrated by his capture. 'What a miserable failure,' he said to Ellis. 'I wouldn't have cared if I had broken off his legs. There ought to have been about 500 of us present. We certainly did not expect this.'

In court the defendants expressed their regret, yet claimed they had a justified grievance and were trying to protect the reputation of their college. 'We should not mind the dog being there at all, but what we do object to is the part of the inscription which states that the dog was done to death in the University College,' said Saunders. 'We are always being taunted by the others about it.'

Magistrate Taylor said he was surprised that such conduct should be proved against 'educated young gentlemen', but Battersea council had thought it right to erect the monument and it was his duty to support that action. If 500 of them had come down, as had been the plan, then the disturbance could have become 'a public riot'. Although the inscription might be distasteful to the defendants, he said, there was no doubt that there were 'hundreds and thousands' of men and women in the country who would thoroughly endorse the action of the council. He fined them each £5 plus ten shillings for the damage, and warned them that if any more medical students were brought before him charged with similar conduct he would send them to prison for two months with hard labour.

At last the dog was back in the news. An eager public seized on the new development and the newspapers jumped at the chance to retell the whole saga. 'To say that the vivisecting medical profession hates the brown dog of Battersea is to put the case mildly,' said the Morning Leader of 21 November 1907. 'Why is it that students cannot comport themselves in a manner befitting their station in life?' wondered the Birmingham Daily Mail. 'The fact that their disorderly conduct is often regarded with a lenient eye by magistrates is probably a contributory cause. The latest escapade is one that will earn the reprobation of all good citizens.'

The University College Union Magazine took a more relaxed view, producing a light half hearted rhyming account of the incident accompanied by a cartoon of a bandaged and bruised brown dog asking 'what next I wonder?' But it also cautioned: 'This tale, like all tales, bears a moral/Your angry passions must be curbed/If with the law you would not quarrel/Let LYING dogs rest undisturbed'.

The BMJ defended the students up to a point, claiming a 'mighty fuss' had been made about the attack, and castigating Taylor for his 'extraordinary' assertion that the memorial was perfectly legitimate. But it also dissociated itself from their actions and admitted that 'it would have been more dignified to leave the work of art alone'. For the most part the students' ill-conceived venture won them widespread disapproval, even from those who had vigorously opposed the memorial. The South Western Star called their actions 'indefensible', and warned that their status as Edwardian gentlemen gave them no special privileges. 'There cannot be one standard of conduct for the ordinary individual and another for those whose parents or friends are rich enough to pay the fees

A 1907 Daily Express cartoon celebrates the first attack on the dog

of the medical schools,' it said. 'Yesterday's prisoners ought to have been sent to gaol instead of being visited with what to them is a trumpery fine.'

The diarist of the Wandsworth Borough News, who was staunchly unsympathetic to the dog's cause and had hitherto tried to ignore the controversy, was disgusted by 'the unseemly and inexpressibly silly attitude' of the students. 'To have a grievance – or to think you have one – and to try and redress it by legitimate methods is one thing, and riotous disorder, involving damage to property, is another,' he said. 'There is no excuse for this, and the young bloods who were fined last week got what they deserved.'

Reaction at the council was predictably stormy. The finance committee agreed to convey its appreciation to the two off-duty officers who had 'saved' the dog, although councillor George Rees used the vote to challenge what he felt was becoming a general perception that the people of Battersea were in favour of the memorial. All councillors, he said, were against the action of the students (at which point an anonymous voice muttered 'not all') but it was misleading the people of London to be told that the majority of Battersea residents were happy with the brown dog. Municipal reformers felt the council had made too much fuss about the damage, and objected to the court statement of town clerk Marcus Wilkins that repairing the memorial would require a new moulding at a cost of £400-£500. Under persistent and sarcastic questioning from councillor Henry Bigden, Wilkins conceded that the damage covered an area no bigger than his little finger nail.

The South Western Star, with the benefit of a week's thought, now changed its tune and decided the council was making a meal of the incident. 'The brown dog episode, having ceased to be serious, has now become amusing,' it claimed on 29 November 1907. 'One can afford to laugh at the students, at their inexperience and their want of commonsense. The Battersea authorities, however, continue to be in a state of continuous peturbation.' The students' failure, it said, had been taken badly in some quarters. One well known local doctor had told the paper he saw the affair as proof of the 'utter degeneration' of junior doctors. 'Two policemen took 10 students,' he moaned. 'I can remember the time when it was more than 10 policemen could do to take one student. The Anglo-Saxon race is played out.'

The November 1907 attack was indeed a minor and rather comical incident, yet it was significant nonetheless. There was little damage to speak of, and the students undoubtedly bungled their best opportunity to destroy the dog. But their foray into the Latchmere Estate ensured that what had threatened to become a fading dispute sparked back into life. Had Lister and friends decided to stay home that evening, it is possible the brown dog would have settled into relative obscurity. As it was they lit the blue touch paper for further events. As Lister said later: 'Our little attempt, though unsuccessful in deed, succeeded in principle far more than any of us had dreamed, for our protest roused the whole college to a realisation of the insulting and slanderous libel which this statue bears. Students of every faculty rallied to our standard.'

the 'riots'

students take to the streets ... effigy burning and fights with the police ... a showdown in Trafalgar Square ... the dog survives unscathed

THE MEDICAL STUDENTS of London were incensed by the outcome of Lister's failed expedition. Aggrieved that their representatives had not only been caught, but fined and threatened with severe punishment, they now needed little encouragement to take their protest onto the streets.

Within a few hours of the trial verdict, a knot of angry students appeared spontaneously in Tottenham Court Road, where they lifted off and carried away a well known wooden figure of a highland snuff-taker that adorned the doorway of a large furniture shop. The snuff-taker had started life as a tobacconist's sign but had become something of a college mascot and was often swept away when the students were acting-up in town. They paraded it through the streets on a wheelbarrow and carried it to the roof of University College Hospital in Gower Street where, in the fading light, they fixed it to the flagstaff and danced around a bonfire in the quadrangle.

The events of that evening proved a valuable warm-up for a larger scale demonstration the following day, Friday 22 November 1907, when hundreds of medical students from Guy's Hospital, King's College, Charing Cross Hospital and Middlesex Hospital made their way from all directions to University College. Shortly after 2pm the quadrangle in front of the college was crowded with a mob of excited male students laying the college to siege and chanting 'down with the brown dog' and 'we want the guy' – a reference to an effigy of magistrate Taylor which was being prepared behind the scenes.

The college authorities hurriedly locked the outside gates but latecomers still managed to swarm in over the railings and into the open space, to the cheers of those already inside. When the guy appeared – 'a hideous object, life-size ... with the hair plastered back over its forehead in close imitation of the style adopted by Mr Taylor' – a huge roar went up, and students locked inside the college forced their way out by the doors and windows.

With Taylor's bizarre effigy up front and others carrying home-made figures of furry brown dogs on poles, the excited mob left the college to collect reinforcements, reaching 1,000 strong by the time they had passed through Tottenham Court Road and singing loudly: 'Lets hang Paul Taylor on a sour apple tree as we go marching on.' They progressed unhindered as they moved on towards King's College in the Strand via Oxford Street and Leicester Square. But at Trafalgar Square the police, who until now had been caught on the hop by the demonstration, barred the way. As they tried to break up the march, hundreds of students broke through the cordon and ran down Chandos Place towards the Strand, stopping the traffic, scattering shoppers and startling old ladies. An enormous crowd of opportunistic onlookers followed at their tail as they marched as far as St Clement Danes church, where a small force of police again tried – in vain – to stop them.

It was probably here that some of the students ran into Edward Ford, who chronicled his surprise encounter a year later in a pamphlet called *The Brown Dog and His memorial*. Ignorant of the brown dog affair after returning from a long period abroad, Ford was walking in the Strand when he was surrounded by a crowd of excited young men shouting and singing. 'Having had my nose brushed with a fluffy toy animal carried aloft by one of the youths, I naturally inquired the cause of this unusual attention to peaceful pedestrians,' he recounted. 'By way of an answer I was swept along the pavement and tightly enclosed in the midst of what was apparently a party of medical students inspired by a common grievance and intent on airing it to the whole world.'

Having extricated himself from the throng, he sought further information from a nearby policeman who, if Ford is to be believed, delivered an explanation worthy of the most clichéd cockney music hall copper. 'It's only them brown doggers, sir,' gabbled the officer. 'They's riled because their professor did something to a dawg wot's called vivispection, and the ladies, they stuck up a monument to the dawg in Battersea, and they says it was tortured, and that the professor he broke the law, but them young gentlemen says it's a shame and now the fat's in the fire, sir.'

As the students rushed off, they sung a song which was to serve them well for some time. Put to the tune of the *Old Brown Jug*, it boasted a chorus of 'Ha ha ha! Hee hee hee! Little brown dog how we hate thee' and, according to Ford, ran as follows:

> As we go walking after dark,
> We turn our steps to Latchmere Park,
> And there we see, to our surprise,
> A little brown dog that stands and lies

If we had a dog which told such fibs,
We'd ply a whip about his ribs,
To tan him well we would not fail,
For carrying such a monstrous tale

Little brown dogs may sit and beg,
But they must not pull the public's leg,
And if put-up stories shock the town,
The authorities ought to pull them down

The bulk of the students rushed round to the left of the church and had arrived inside the courtyard of King's College before the authorities had time to close the gates. Once inside, Taylor's effigy was fixed against some iron railings in the centre of the quad and set alight. The jubilant spectators waved their hats and sticks in the air, to loud shouts of 'down with Paul Taylor the unjust judge'. The guy refused to burn with any vigour, so the ringleaders lifted it up and took it to the nearby Thames, where the remains were thrown into the water amid hisses and groans. With the effigy disposed of, the mob marched across the river to Guy's Hospital before returning to University College, where a more organised police detachment of 400 was by now waiting for them.

The police barred the entrance but the students had achieved what they set out to do, and after some further chanting and singing they dispersed, according to the sympathetic London Evening Standard, 'feeling fully satisfied with the success of the day's proceedings'.

In Battersea, meanwhile, the Latchmere Estate had been thrown into a state of siege as the local police, hearing news of the west end disturbances, moved every available constable into the area as a precautionary measure. Mounted officers patrolled Battersea Park Road while large numbers of men on foot surrounded the monument and a detachment of determined council workmen stood by armed with brooms. But nothing happened. There were no arrests either in Battersea or the West End, despite some fairly fierce confrontations as the police tried to stop the guy being burned, and there had been few negative reactions on the street, save for some flak from cabmen and bus drivers whose progress had been blocked.

Reaction in the national press was rather more hostile. The Daily Graphic claimed the demonstration was 'about as stupid and in as bad taste as could possibly be conceived', especially when it came to the parading of dogs on poles. 'One would have supposed that students with any respect for their profession would have regarded it (the brown dog) as a humble creature that gave its life for the benefit of humanity, and would have treated its memory accordingly,' it raged. 'But these are ideas that probably do not occur to the heroes of yesterday's exhibition.'

Most newspaper commentators called for a swift end to the students' antics, yet, as the Yorkshire Herald observed the following day, the brown dog memorial had 'aroused the ire of every Bob Sawyer in London' and on the evening after the effigy burning, Saturday 23 November, there were further demonstrations involving about 150 students in Piccadilly Circus. Three medical students, Samuel Middlebrook of Norwood, Emanuel De Meza of Highgate, and Arthur Fuelings of Crouch Hill were subsequently charged with breach of the peace offences at Marlborough Street court, and were bound over for six months in the sum of £5. No sooner had they left court than a gathering of students from various colleges assembled for a noisy lunchtime demonstration at the gates of University College.

Small-scale disturbances continued throughout the week, culminating in drunken scenes on the Friday night of 30 November, when around 100 young men held a rowdy midnight demonstration in Leicester Square. Three veterinary students – Robert Goodyear of Kentish Town plus two brothers, Dobbs and Horace Sewell of Eton Square, were charged with being drunk and disorderly and obstructing the police after waving a stuffed Irish terrier in the air and striking passers by with it. The stuffed dog was confiscated and produced in court, where the Bow Street magistrate, Sir Albert de Rutzen, said it was a pity to see three young men who probably had successful careers before them in such a position. He fined each five shillings, and bound Goodyear over to be of good behaviour. The stuffed dog was ordered to be kept by the police until further notice.

University College officials found themselves trying to tread a thin line between condemning the students' actions and justifying their anger at the brown dog memorial. After the effigy burning incident they arranged a meeting at which the provost, Dr Gregory Foster, appointed a committee of students to defray the cost of damages incurred during the first two days of demonstrations, including the loss of 'the ancient college wheelbarrow' which had been used to transport the highland snuff-taker.

The move eased some of the external pressure on the college to take control of its students, yet there was equally strong internal pressure for college officials to take a much stronger stance on the memorial. Students had already been lobbying their MP, Sir Philip Magnus (who specifically represented London University), and a meeting of the college's council on 3 December was sent a belligerent statement by Stuart Willcox, president of the college's Union Society, promising that students in London 'will not rest until the reference to University College is removed from the inscription on the dog'. Willcox acknowledged that the demonstrations had been 'harmful to the college' but said he was confident 'that there will be renewed disturbances' until action was taken. The council told the students it would seek further legal opinion, though probably more in hope than expectation, given that it had already taken advice on the inscription a year earlier and had drawn a blank.

The legal explorations could not, in any case, be completed quickly enough to avert a much more serious demonstration several days later. Willcox's promise of 'renewed disturbances' had not been an empty one, and on Tuesday 10 December, the centre of London erupted in noisy confrontation.

Unlike the impromptu gatherings of the previous two weeks, the 10 December demonstration had been planned more openly, and there had been much advance talk of it in the newspapers. On the day, street vendors were even selling souvenir paper handkerchiefs which read: 'Brown dog's inscription is a lie, and the statuette an insult to the London University. In commemoration of the procession of students from the "square". Another brown dog demonstration, Tuesday December 10, 1907.'

Howard Lister and friends had decided to capitalise on the fact that thousands of potentially sympathetic Oxbridge students would be in town for the day to watch the annual varsity rugby match between Oxford and Cambridge universities. Hoping that their numbers would be swelled by excited and vociferous day trippers, they arranged for a march to Trafalgar Square to begin outside the Queen's Club in West Kensington, where the match was being played. When sufficient protesters had gathered, the main body would descend on Trafalgar Square while a more violently-inclined detachment would march south to Battersea, where the plan was to smash down the dog and throw it into the Thames.

The response from the Oxbridge rugby watchers was not all that Lister had hoped for, due in part to the deterrent factor of a large police presence outside the Queen's Club. Yet after the match had finished at 3.45pm, there were still enough of them – when they mingled with the London students – to create a crowd of more than 250 outside the meeting point at Baron's Court underground station. One 150 strong group, some waving rattles, marched off noisily along Hammersmith Road towards Trafalgar Square while the rest set off for Battersea.

Those bound for the West End were headed by two men bearing the by-now familiar brown dog dummies on poles, and a banner reading 'nine Taylors make a man'. They had acquired a mounted police escort early on, but continued to pick up supporters and sightseers along the route, including 30 who joined as they passed the grounds of St Paul's School and, more briefly, a busking Scottish piper.

The march grew rowdier and more menacing as the throng passed through Kensington towards Hyde Park Corner, where there was much barking and shouting as the students walked by St George's Hospital. In fact police decided that things had become so disorderly by this stage that they charged the marchers, scattering them into small groups and chasing most of them down Piccadilly. Others who had been separated from the main body evaded the police by taking alternative routes to Trafalgar Square, some of them by bus.

As they all appeared within striking distance of the square they were joined by a large group of other students, perhaps from Guy's Hospital, who had emerged from the north side of Northumberland Avenue. Most ran in successive waves straight towards Nelson's Column, while some who had arrived near the National Gallery as the winter darkness fell at around 4.45pm were temporarily pushed away by a police reception committee.

As midweek meetings were not allowed in Trafalgar Square by law, the police were obliged to try to prevent the gathering. Despite their best efforts, however, most of the students – enforced by a significant section of the interested general public – had managed to get to the square by early evening and a sizeable, excited crowd of around 400 people assembled around the base of Nelson's Column. Several of the student leaders scrambled onto the pedestal, although each was pulled down by the police before they could make a speech.

In an effort to gain control of the situation, mounted police decided on a charge, moving in at about 5.45pm to make several arrests as students fought with police on foot. As the first arrest was made, a large crowd broke off to follow the victim to Cannon Row police station, where they refused to move from the area around Scotland Yard. Mounted officers came to the aid of ordinary constables and the crowd made a second rush back to Nelson's Column, trying again to get onto the pedestal. There were further arrests as the swelling mob threatened to overwhelm the 100 or so police.

There was another police charge and at least ten minutes of serious disorder, followed by turbulent scenes all around the area as students

the 'riots'

A stylised version of the 'riots' from Ford's pamphlet on the brown dog affair

scattered down various adjoining streets. A police presence was sent down Whitehall to deal with a break-away group wielding a brown dog dummy, eventually breaking it up on the steps leading to Waterloo Bridge before they could get to King's College. As more arrests were made between 6pm and 7pm, the police began to gain the upper hand and the square slowly started to clear. No longer able to act as a single body, the students had lost their momentum and began drifting off in small groups, either to go home or to seek further entertainment in the pubs, restaurants, music halls and theatres of the West End. The Empire Theatre became crowded with demonstrators, many of whom were ejected for rowdiness. By 8pm police had withdrawn from the square and normality had returned, although officers continued to position themselves in large numbers on various streets around the West End as their superiors drafted in an extra 300 constables in case of further flare-ups.

They were wise to do so, because after midnight the crowds began to reassemble, this time around Leicester Square and Piccadilly Circus. Refuelled by drink, the students sung and cheered in small knots then formed into a group of around 120, making their way back down St Martin's Lane to Trafalgar Square, where they were met by a large force of police, including 15 on horseback. There were two arrests as the officers tried to disperse them, but the confrontation was better-natured than earlier in the evening and the crowd had filtered away by 1am. The bulk of the police were allowed off duty at 2am.

Exciting as the confrontations had been in Trafalgar Square, the more significant action had been expected in Battersea, where police had been waiting for the 100 students to make their attack on the memorial. For the students, however, the bold foray south of the river turned into a humiliating retreat. Throughout the week rumours had been circulating Battersea that a 1000-strong mob would come to the Latchmere Estate. Lister had actually been banking on 300 to do the job and although only a third of that number appeared, the police had decided to be prepared for all eventualities. The local superintendent called out all available men, saturating Battersea Park Road and its surrounding streets with police on horse and foot, guarding all approaches to the recreation ground, setting up cordons around the memorial (which had already been under special guard for the past three weeks) and positioning reserves on every spare piece of ground. Battersea was well protected; altogether 250 uniformed men were on duty, supplemented by a large force of plain clothes detectives acting as scouts.

The students had at first felt heartened when their own scouts had reported back that all was quiet at the recreation ground. But most of the police had been lying in ambush inside a huge shed, and when the students finally reached Latchmere in two groups just after dusk at 5pm they soon realised they were hopelessly outnumbered and outmanoeuvred. There was a short, token struggle during which one enterprising student managed to slip in close to the fountain, but his colleagues found it impossible to pierce the cordons across the paths leading to the memorial and, realising their mission was now futile, they broke up into small parties as they sheltered in doorways from the mounted police.

Here they came up against a second, unexpected force: the local people, who began pelting the retreating intruders with mud and street sweepings. Hostile, jeering crowds of local youths 'attacked everyone they imagined to be students' said the Standard, and 'more than one harmless young man on his way home was covered with mud from head to foot before the youngsters could be induced to desist'.

Finding themselves hemmed in on the one side by angry locals and on the other by police, most of the students decided to beat a hasty retreat, but became involved in more skirmishes as they ran past the heavily-guarded Anti-Vivisection Hospital. One student injured himself after falling from a tram, much to the delight of locals who stood and shouted jubilantly: 'That's the brown dog's revenge!' His friends tried to carry him to the 'Anti-Vivi' for treatment but a group of local workers barred the door and refused to let him enter.

Some of the more determined students returned later to hang about in twos and threes for the remainder of the evening, although the police kept them on the move and prevented the formation of any larger gatherings. All officers remained on alert until 2am, with patrols ordering all suspicious looking people to move on. Latchmere Estate residents kept their eyes open, too; an unfortunate pair of young local men passing the recreation ground later that night were mistaken for students by a crowd of boys, who pelted them with mud. They ran off with the boys in hot pursuit, and were kept under constant fire until they managed to take refuge in Lavender Hill police station.

There were no arrests at the Battersea debacle, although several students appeared at Bow Street court on the following day for their part in the Trafalgar Square disturbances. Sympathizers surrounded the court entrance as a dozen were charged with disorderly conduct and resisting the police. Prosecution counsel said the police were becoming 'somewhat weary' of the brown dog disturbances and were concerned that the

the 'riots'

leniency displayed in previous cases had been misplaced. But the magistrate ignored calls for tougher sentencing: he imposed fines of 40 shillings on Robert Overton, aged 21, Llewellyn Rhys Warburton (20), George Carr (18), Arthur Keyworth (24), Harry Burdett (20) and Sidney Whitehead (17). He bound over Sydney White (19), and Harry Coombes (30).

Frederick Simpson (23), and Christopher Dudgeon (20), were fined heftier sums of £3 each for fighting with police after Dudgeon's arrest, but Alexander Bowley, a 20-year-old Cambridge undergraduate arrested for 'barking like a dog', and 'otherwise behaving in a disorderly manner' was discharged when the prosecution agreed the case against him was of insufficient gravity. Frederick Grange (23), a corn merchant from Tring, was also discharged. He had joined the mêlée after dining with his father and a friend at a farmer's dinner in The Criterion and was alleged to have shouted: 'It will take 40 policemen to take me.'

The events of 10 December shocked the public and prompted dramatic front page headlines such as 'Tumult in Trafalgar Square'. The Daily Telegraph said the scenes were 'riotous', the Daily Chronicle called them a 'students' riot'. They were certainly the most disorderly incidents since the first attack on the memorial six weeks previously, although whether they could be classified as a riot is another matter. The point is not entirely academic, as with the passage of time the disturbances of that night, lumped together with the other marches and confrontations of the previous few weeks, have become known as 'the brown dog riots'.

On the bare criteria of the Oxford English Dictionary's definition of a riot ('a violent disturbance to the peace; an outbreak of active lawlessness or disorder among the populace') then the Trafalgar Square fighting, and perhaps even the effigy burning at King's College, could reasonably have been described as such. But on a wider consideration of contemporary accounts, it is difficult to come to the conclusion that either event truly merited the description.

Although the Trafalgar Square disorder and the effigy burning may both have been alarming to confused passers-by, no property was damaged, there was no prolonged fighting, there were only a handful of arrests (mainly for minor offences), and the police were in control for almost the entire time. The threat of violence was serious, yet outside of a few fist-fights it failed to escalate. Any march involving several charges by mounted police is clearly worthy of attention, but compared with other violent confrontations which have taken place in the square – before and since – the 10 December affair was small beer, little more than a protest

Guilty brown doggers (from left): Simpson, Dudgeon, Warburton, Overton, Whitehead, Carr, Burdett, Keyworth and Coombes

march which got out of hand. The Daily News probably had it about right when it talked of 'a miniature riot' and although 'the Brown dog disturbances' may not sound as dramatic as the 'brown dog riots' the phrase has a greater ring of truth.

The disturbances at King's College and Trafalgar Square were, on the other hand, not as trifling as some of the more conservative newspapers tried to make out. Much of their language was clearly influenced by the social status of those who took part in the demonstrations; they talked not of fighting but of 'scuffles', 'good natured conflict', 'horseplay', and 'high jinks' – phrases which they were unlikely to have used if the demonstration had involved trade unionists, suffragettes or home rulers, especially if they were attacking the police.

There was undoubtedly a high-spirited element to aspects of the demonstrations, yet the picture painted by some newspapers of a 'rag'-style adventure is unlikely to have borne much relation to reality. The students were, after all, angry enough to take to the streets and to risk imprisonment – and at Trafalgar Square were willing to use violence. Ford had been rather amused by his first encounter with the 'brown doggers' and had decided to join the Trafalgar Square march as an interested eyewitness. But he had speedily abandoned his mission when he realised the demeanour of the crowd. 'A feeling of uneasiness came over me as I watched the expressions on the faces of the young haters of the brown dog,' he said. 'I have seen young men use fisticuffs in their clamour for the recognition of the rights of the oppressed ... but here I saw no such light. The power behind these crowds of riotous students lacked signs which are inseparable from any movement springing from the spiritually progressive instincts of humanity. This was an ugly onslaught without the inspiration which makes ugly onslaughts beautiful.'

Riot or not, the newspapers went to town during the next few days,

the 'riots'

featuring large line drawings of the arrested students supported by photographs of the infamous fountain and condemnation of the students' behaviour. The Daily Graphic summed up the stand-point of most pro-vivisection newspapers when it claimed the students had a valid grievance against an inscription that was causing 'turbulence and martyrdom' but warned the 'high-spirited young men' involved to exercise self-control. 'The general public is rather sceptical of sincerity when it takes the form of undignified scrambles between medical students and the police,' it said. 'This is all to the bad for the cause the agitators have at heart.'

The anti-vivisectionist papers, by contrast, had been delighted by the turn of events. The Star actually thanked the students for organizing 'another magnificent advertisement of the brown dog and the cause which it represents,' arguing that the demonstrators 'are doing more for the anti-vivisection movement than all the anti-vivisectionists have ever done, for they are making people think and talk about the hidden cruelties which are perpetrated in the name of scientific research'.

The Daily News took a similar line, claiming that as an opponent of vivisection it 'could wish for nothing better than that the medical students of London should continue the form of propaganda which they have recently adopted'. The Morning Leader said the public had been given 'an object lesson in the spirit of the men who are now being trained for our future doctors,' and the Christian Commonwealth came to the conclusion that 'there is a sense in which we are not at all sorry that the medical students of London should have given the general public so striking a demonstration of the spirit they are of. Law-abiding citizens who never knew, nor cared to know much about vivisection know now at least, what it produces.'

December copies of the University College union magazine, which normally made a loss, were sold out. Yet even its pages presented only a subdued, slightly jokey justification of the students' actions. Only the BMJ made a determined defence of the Trafalgar Square scenes, deploring the disturbances 'on the part of lads who should know better' but complaining of 'the fuss made by certain newspapers about the "rioting" of a handful of boys'. The memorial, it said, 'is a standing provocation to young men naturally high-spirited and proud of the profession which it is the business of these agitators to vilify'.

The BMJ may have been the most outspoken supporter of the students but it was by no means out on a limb when it came to condemning the brown dog memorial. Even some prominent anti-vivisectionists, such as the writer, former University of London student and Battersea resident GK Chesterton, felt the fountain was unnecessarily provocative. 'No-one seems really to have troubled about the actual ethics underlying the students' outbreak,' wrote Chesterton in the Illustrated London News. 'The idea behind the students' action was, I think, this quite rational idea, right or wrong, that a public street and a public monument were being used against a public decision and a public morality.

'The mere fact that certain people are humanitarians and have a reasonable ideal ought not to permit them to erect brown dogs in the streets of Battersea. I know many people of the noblest moral nature who have really persuaded themselves that the eating of any kind of animal food is cruel and obscene, cannibalism. They meet me, they shake me by the hand, they ask me to give them lectures, but the fact remains that they must, from their own point of view, quite rightly regard me as wicked for eating haddock for breakfast. But I must confess that I should be annoyed if I walked out one morning into Battersea Park and found a monument to the haddock, in a pathetic and arresting attitude, with an inscription underneath saying: "This is the martyred haddock, murdered to make the bestial breakfast of GK Chesterton, who lives in the mansion just over the way." I should object to being made the object of a public rebuke when I had no reason to believe that it came from the public.'

Chesterton's observations went to the heart of the students'

Sydney White (second from left) is forcibly persuaded by his student colleagues to pose for the cameras outside Bow Street Court

objections, as one of the arrested University College men, anonymously speaking to the Daily Chronicle, confirmed. 'We don't mind the statue itself in the least,' he said, 'but we do bar the words which state that the brown dog was atrociously done to death at this institution. It is a quite gratuitous insult born of hysteria'. Even Coleridge admitted that if the fountain 'had concerned some other question in which I was not interested, I might hold a different opinion as to its suitability'. Pro-vivisectionists such as the surgeon Stephen Paget, secretary of the Association for the Advancement of Medicine by Research and son of Sir James Paget, who had vainly tried to persuade Queen Victoria to drop her opposition to vivisection, used the spectre of the 'riots' as evidence that the inscription was an incitement to commit a breach of the peace. 'The students are justly angry at false witness borne against University College, and some excuse may be found for the attempt to smash the memorial,' he wrote in The Times.

The disturbances may therefore have done the image of the students or vivisectors little good, but they did increase the pressure on Battersea council – already under fire for increasing the rates to pay for more municipal schemes – to do something about what many saw as a needlessly provocative inscription. 'Events of the past few days make it apparent that Battersea ... is becoming notorious by the action of the borough council in allowing the erection of the monument to the brown dog' said one correspondent in the South Western Star. 'Artistically the monument is about as mean as it could be. The sting, however, lies in the inscription, which surely should be removed, as many consider it to be an insult to a noble and humane profession. Apart from this, a monument which requires such expensive guarding becomes a public nuisance. Is part of the increased rate to be expended in this manner? If so I might suggest it would be cheaper to construct an iron cage similar to the one in the Tower for the protection of the crown jewels.'

Increasingly the brown dog was becoming a stick with which to beat the council for its radical initiatives. In the wider debate about the morality of vivisection the Trafalgar Square scenes probably lost the vivisectionists some ground, yet on the narrow issue of whether the memorial should be allowed to remain in place, they could well have helped their cause. The students may not have got close enough to physically damage the memorial, but metaphorically they had dealt it a few more hammer blows, and they were ready now to move into a new phase of protest.

more trouble

students clash with anti-vivisectionists ... mass meetings support the dog
... complaints about policing costs ... first moves to destroy monument

THE NEW SPHERE of activity took the students off the streets and into the capital's meeting halls, where they attempted to disrupt a series of anti-vivisectionist debates inspired by the renewed national prominence of the brown dog memorial.

The first meeting took place on a Wednesday evening, 11 December 1907, at Acton Central Hall in west London, the day after the Trafalgar Square disturbances. The gathering had been arranged by the middle class ladies of the Ealing and Acton Anti-Vivisection Society, who had invited prominent figures in the movement, including Lind-af-Hageby, to speak in favour of the memorial. At the scheduled start time of 8pm, the left hand side of the hall had been occupied by 200 students, several of them armed with rattles, others with trumpets and mouth organs, and one wielding a huge mask representing the head of the brown dog.

The invasion had not been unexpected; the Daily Chronicle reported that 'all sorts of horrid rumours had been terrifying the Ealing boudoirs and drawing rooms' during the preceding few days – but the ladies were still shocked at how quickly their meeting degenerated into pandemonium. A stink bomb and some fire crackers were let off as the first speaker took the floor, forcing several women to flee the hall altogether, and by the time Lind-af-Hageby rose to talk there had already been some significant skirmishing between the students and stewards.

For Lind-af-Hageby the events of the past few weeks had injected into her life just the kind of excitement she thrived on. She had returned briefly to Sweden after the death of her mother in 1905, but for the most part had remained in London since the brown dog trial and was now about to enter what John Vyvyan called 'the most active and creative period of her life'.

Back in demand as a speaker and a figure of controversy, she threw herself into the fray, relishing the cut and thrust of debate and proving herself one of the few anti-vivisectionist speakers able to cope with the haranguing tactics of her opponents. The BMJ derided her 'vixenish

more trouble

'The lively student seems to be dividing his favours between the brown dog and the suffragette' – The Tatler's view of the student protests

oratory' yet there was little doubt she was able to hold her own on the platform and at times was capable of giving much better than she got.

In the sulphurous, smoky atmosphere of the Acton meeting she responded pluckily to the shouts of the boisterous students, castigating one man for blowing sarcastic kisses at her (a gesture which greatly outraged the elderly ladies in the audience) and fighting on through the noisy heckling. Several students stood on chairs to ask questions as more stink bombs went off, clearing a huge space in the centre of the hall. Lind-af-Hageby soldiered on despite verbal abuse covering what one newspaper called 'the whole gamut of hospital slang', but when the protesters began singing their brown dog song, blowing trumpets and waving their rattles, she was unable to make her voice heard above the disorder, and sat down to await developments.

Lind-af-Hageby's enforced retirement proved the catalyst for some heated and angry altercations. In scenes of disorder which would not have looked out of place in a Laurel and Hardy film, a huge free fight followed as the frustrated stewards stepped in to eject the protesters. 'For 20 minutes men swayed to and fro, chairs crunched and crashed, coats were torn and collars shredded into ribbons,' said the Daily Chronicle. 'Every now and then a thud announced that another student had been flung into the street.' Whistles were blown, students hit stewards with walking sticks, hats were trampled underfoot, women screamed, and the hall echoed to the sounds of 'the wrenching of timber and convulsive breathing'.

Relative order was only restored when a detachment of police arrived, expelling the students and arresting one medical student, Terence Buller of Stockwell, who was bailed out by his companions. After releasing their man at the police station the demonstrators tried to re-enter the hall, but found their passage barred by the police, so they marched down the Uxbridge Road eastwards towards Shepherd's Bush, throwing aside roadworks paraphernalia and road signs as they went.

After a walk of about a mile the mob began to run, followed closely by a group of panting constables who, finding themselves outpaced, decided they could only continue the chase by boarding an electric tram. The students ran on for a while longer, then stopped and doubled back towards Acton as the police shot by on their commandeered vehicle. By the time they had dismounted and run back along the Uxbridge Road their quarry had changed tactics again and were now walking back towards them, content that they had given their tormentors the runaround. The students continued to progress in fairly good order to Shepherd's Bush Green, where they disappeared into the tube station and dispersed. Buller was fined 20 shillings plus costs at Acton Police Court the following day for butting a policeman in the stomach and hitting him in the face.

Undaunted by her experiences in Acton, Lind-af-Hageby accepted

more trouble

another invitation to speak five days later on Monday 16 December, this time at Caxton Hall not far from Parliament Square, on the thorny subject of 'vivisection and medical students'. The Caxton Hall event had been designated an all-ticket affair in an attempt to avoid a repeat of the Acton scenes, and was heavily guarded by several dozen stewards brought in from Battersea. Nonetheless about 50 students had, by fair means or foul, managed to get tickets. They sat relatively quietly under the suspicious eyes of the stewards, until Lind-af-Hageby began to make her speech.

When Lind-af-Hageby mentioned the name of the magistrate Paul Taylor a storm of boos and hisses went up, met with counter cries of 'serves you right you young cads!' then some further interruptions, some rattle waving and a rendition of the brown dog anthem. Lind-af-Hageby hit back at the students, claiming they had 'far exceeded the boundaries of legitimate youthful hilarity' and had descended 'into brutality'. Her words caused uproar, putting an effective end to the meeting as more stink bombs went off and a gaggle of students who had climbed onto the roof of an adjoining hotel began banging on the windows and ventilation pipes. Amid the confusion, Howard Lister was allowed onto the platform and seemed to apologise for the recent disturbances, but no sooner had he made his speech than a door burst open at the back of the platform and a dozen students charged into the meeting amid great cheers.

The chairman John Baird abandoned the debate as women fled for the exits and the Battersea men moved in to quell the demonstrators. Blows were exchanged, but this time the stewards posed a more formidable threat, and within a short time the students had decided a quick exit was the best course of action. They moved out of the hall, singing loudly, and marched off towards Trafalgar Square. Before they reached their goal they were headed off in Parliament Street by a dozen constables and, as more police reinforcements arrived, an attempt to hold an impromptu meeting on Horse Guards Parade came to nothing.

Press reaction to the new indoor 'riots' was no more favourable than it had been to the outdoor disturbances; there were numerous leader comments critical of the behaviour of what the Manchester Guardian called 'very poor specimens of the student class'. Yet most newspapers continued to argue that the further disorder only underlined the folly of Battersea council's decision to accept the memorial – that it showed the urgent need for a change to the memorial's inscription, if not its complete removal. Battersea was not endearing itself to the establishment on many fronts; as the Acton meeting took place the conservative papers were already in a lather over its plans to impose a 3d supplementary rate to finance a public works programme aimed at creating jobs for the unemployed. They were not going to allow their unease about the character of the disturbances to detract from their determination to nail the council's progressive councillors.

Pressure had come, too, from a hitherto unexpected source: the police. Two days after the Trafalgar Square disturbances the mayor of Battersea had been sent a letter from the Commissioner of Police, Sir Edward Henry, suggesting that the public cost of protecting the monument was becoming prohibitive. 'Sooner or later, unless special protection is provided, it will be either disfigured or destroyed,' the letter said. Twenty-four-hour protection already required the services of four police officers to guard the dog from 4pm until early morning, plus two additional constables to keep a look out for the rest of the day, at a cost of at least £700 per year. 'In the circumstances the Commissioner is compelled to inquire whether, if your council desire that the statue remain in its present position, they will be prepared to defray the cost of such special services of police'.

Battersea progressives were flabbergasted by such an unusual request. So flabbergasted, in fact, that more than a few appeared to reconsider their position for the first time, and one of their number, aghast at the prospect of having to increase the rates even further to pay for the monument, is said to have suggested encasing it in a cage of hardened steel and surrounding it with a barbed wire fence. Others initially felt, as the South Western Star later argued, that 'no brown dog, alive or dead, is worth the cost and trouble'. Yet within a day or two the surprise had turned to indignation.

'We were simply amazed at the Commissioner's letter,' progressive councillor John Archer told the Daily Mail. 'You might as well ask a neighbourhood where burglaries are frequent to pay the expense of the detectives who scour the country to apprehend the thieves. We already pay in Battersea close on £22,000 per year in police rates and we contend that it is the duty of the police to preserve order. If a set of hooligans from other parts of London come and disturb the peace here, why should we have to pay for their misdeeds?'

The Commissioner's letter eventually came up for discussion at a packed council meeting on Wednesday 8 January 1908, along with a speculative motion from municipal reformer Arthur Runeckles that 'as a matter of good sense, good taste and law and order the un-English libellous and provocative inscription on the little brown dog memorial be removed'.

Two such controversial talking points guaranteed a record attendance of Fleet Street journalists, but the reporters had a frustrating night as the debate on the dog, listed to appear at the end of the agenda, kicked off only a few minutes before the meeting's scheduled finish time of 10.30pm. Councillors were told of a telegram from the Battersea branch of the Operative Bricklayers Society calling on them to 'resist to the utmost' any move to get rid of the memorial or the inscription on it – then heard a similar missive from the Canine Defence League, urging the council to ask the Commissioner of Police 'if Battersea organised a gang similar to the medical hooligans to raid laboratories in order to destroy instruments for animal torture, whether those laboratories would be required to pay for protection from police'. It added: 'To accede to the Commissioner's demand would set up a disastrous precedent that the people must pay twice over to ensure efficient police protection. Battersea should resist this in the interests of all England.'

Runeckles, a publisher, argued that while he did not agree with the medical students' actions the time had come, in the interests of law and order, to replace the inscription on the memorial with some new words 'which would not offend the sensibilities of a large number of people in the borough and the metropolis'. If the inscription remained it would undoubtedly cause even further trouble and expense – and if the progressives refused to pay for its protection the council would end up having to look after the dog itself, with private watchmen. In any case, he warned, there was a chance that the Municipal Reform Party would be coming into power within the next two years, and it was quite on the cards that the inscription as well as the whole fountain would then be removed. Runeckles's motion was seconded, but further consideration was postponed for two weeks as the meeting ran out of time.

With the debate thus agonisingly poised, public discussion of the merits and de-merits of the memorial began to reach a new peak. The following Friday evening, 10 January 1908, the first of three pro-brown dog mass meetings was organised at Battersea Town Hall. Despite the local indignation caused by Sir Edward Henry's letter and a sandwich board advertising campaign asking 'shall Battersea lose its brown dog?' the turnout was disappointing. In fact most of those who attended were stewards – as many as 500 burly local men handpicked for their strength and wearing red ribbons to indicate their socialist sympathies. Every

more trouble

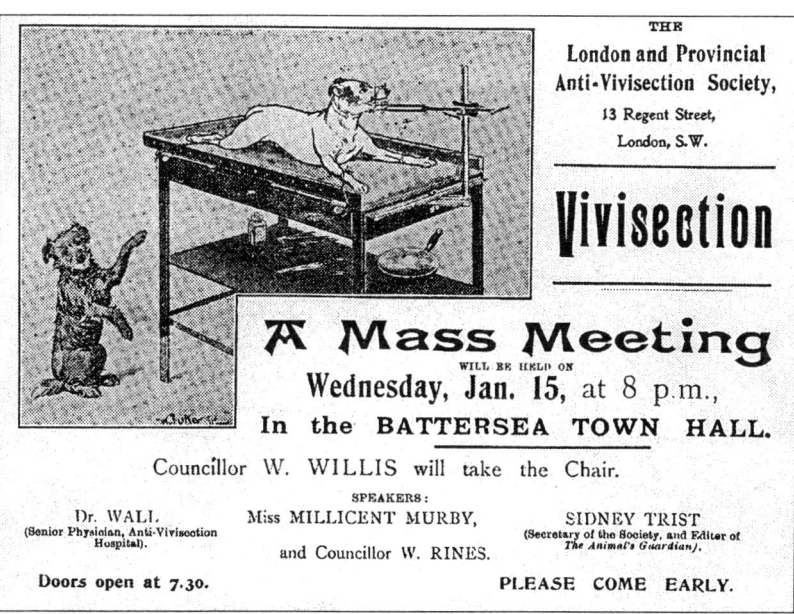

Invitation card to the third Battersea Town Hall meeting

suspected medical student was keenly scrutinised before being seated, whenever possible, between two stewards. Unsurprisingly there was no disorder, although 50 students had been reported to have come armed with sticks.

Most of the formal speech-making was long, dull and more about socialism than the dog itself – and unlike the Acton and Caxton Hall meetings there were very few women present. A resolution to preserve the memorial and condemn vivisection was carried unanimously, after which the students were challenged by the local men 'to come to Battersea on one condition – that they let the defenders of the brown dog know when they are coming'.

The second Battersea Town Hall meeting, on the following Monday 13 January, was a much better attended and far more exciting affair. Lind-af-Hageby was there, supported this time by Charlotte Despard, a posse of local councillors, and Louisa Woodward, the memorial's benefactor. This time the building was packed, the doors were locked and hundreds of people crowded outside, some of them with tickets. 'The talk on the streets was all about the dog, and as I stood watching the stream of working men that filed into the hall long before the appointed time I realised the full moral strength of the anti-vivisection movement which can thus fire thousands of hearts,' said the Daily Chronicle's correspondent. There was a reduced contingent of about 300 stewards, this time wearing green ribbons for Ireland, lining every approach to the hall – although the police were again present in case of disruption. There was little need for them; the stewards performed their job with relish, violently ejecting any students who dared to stir or shout.

Archer moved a resolution in support of the inscription which was supported by Lind-af-Hageby, billed on adverts for the meeting as 'the lady who saw the brown dog vivisected'. Thanks to the stewards she had few interruptions, although several hecklers were bundled out unceremoniously during her speech. Her words drew huge applause. Despard addressed the crowd, according to the South Western Star, 'with that impassioned fire and in that weird manner which leads her admirers to revere her as a prophetess'.

Stephen Paget, now secretary of the newly formed Research Defence Society, and colleague Arthur Capel had been invited to speak against the resolution, but despite the mayor's pleas for a fair hearing the audience quickly became impatient with them, especially when Capel claimed Lind-af-Hageby had proved to be a 'discredited witness' at the brown dog trial. As Capel vainly tried to continue his speech, eyewitness Edward Ford watched as 'the Battersea men filled the hall with the roar of indignant throats', and the speaker hastily retired. The resolution was passed; the South Western Star noted wryly that 'nobody was turned out for interrupting the opposition.'

Two days later there was a third meeting at Battersea Town Hall, again crowded but this time virtually ignored by the students. Former mayor Bill Rines said the council would fight to the last ditch rather than give up the brown dog, and another resolution in support of the monument was passed. Aggressively marshalled and restrictive as they were, the three town hall meetings were a strong show of solidarity which appeared to give the lie to suggestions that the ordinary people of Battersea were embarrassed by the presence of the dog.

Not everyone was impressed; the staunchly anti-dog South Western Star said the meetings were a sham and 'an impertinence' at which 'an army of unemployed has been enrolled to suppress with brutish violence the faintest manifestation of dissent'. The Battersea progressives saw it entirely differently; they believed the meetings had given them a mandate to vote against the removal of the inscription and to rebuff the

Commissioner of Police. 'I think most of us would be more in favour of putting up another brown dog than of taking this one down,' said mayor Fred Worthy, a printer, temperance worker and fervent anti-vivisectionist.

At the resumed council meeting on 22 January 1908 the public gallery was packed to watch the progressives hit back against the Commissioner of Police, whose letter was denounced as 'a shocking confession of incompetence'. In contrast to the long drawn out session a fortnight earlier this was a swifter moving affair, helped along by the eagerness of the municipal reformers (many of whom sat in the council chamber wearing evening dress) to leave early for a formal dinner. Discussion still took two hours, but the progressives were happy to hurry things along and, although master tailor Joseph Ranson, who seconded Runeckles' motion, said that 'as a Britisher' he objected to an inscription effectively written 'by a couple of foreigners', for once some of the municipal reformers wavered in their condemnation of the dog.

The meeting agreed by 29 votes to five 'that the inscription on the memorial being founded on ascertained facts, the council declines to sanction the proposal to remove it, and that the Commissioner of Police be informed in reply to this letter that the care and protection of public monuments is a matter for the police, and that any expense occasioned thereby should be defrayed out of the public rate to which this borough contributes so largely. Also that the council considers more strenuous efforts should be made to suppress any renewal of the organised ruffianism which has recently taken place in the metropolis in connection with the memorial'. It agreed that the Commissioner's letter should be drawn to the attention of the home secretary, Herbert Gladstone.

The progressives had a big enough majority to feel confident that there was no real danger of the inscription being removed, but Runeckles's defeated motion had proved a rallying point for the opponents of the brown dog and they were not about to let the momentum slip. On 6 February Sir Philip Magnus brought the matter to the House of Commons by asking the home secretary how much it was costing the government to protect the memorial – and calling for legislation to ban the erection of monuments with controversial inscriptions in public places.

Magnus assured his fellow MPs that a large body of University of London students were quite prepared to remove the offensive brown dog monument 'free of charge,' but Gladstone played a dead bat to his questions. He outlined the £700 a year costs for the six constables on duty near the dog, and revealed that protection of the monument had used up the equivalent of a day's special service for 27 police inspectors, 55 sergeants and 1,083 constables – plus large numbers of police who had been called out occasionally to deal with related disorders in other parts of London. He was, he admitted, worried that controversial monuments of this type should become fashionable, although he didn't think there were grounds for introducing legislation, nor did he make any suggestion that the monument should be removed.

West Donegal MP Hugh Law argued that the government should extend the Irish Crimes Act to control the students, then the speaker had to bring order when Stirlingshire MP Donald Smeaton caused uproar by trying to argue that the inscription in Battersea 'was neither more nor less than an exact statement of the facts which had been admitted by two professors'.

Magnus later told the Daily Mail he found it 'somewhat peculiar that policemen are specially detailed to guard this private monument,' but the policing argument was a speculative throw of the dice which appeared to gain few genuine converts and, despite the attempts of Sir Edward Henry, could not in any case be acted upon by the home secretary, who had sought advice on the subject from the attorney general.

In his brown dog pamphlet, Ford echoed the views of many at the time when he pointed out that it was part of the Metropolitan Police's job to guard property. 'The private houses in Battersea as well as those near Hyde Park are every night entrusted to the vigilance of special policemen,' he said. 'Though a man or his house may be extremely objectionable to his neighbours, attempts are not generally made to induce the police to leave him unprotected so that his property or life may be attacked. If a band of wild anti-vivisectionists attempted to break into the physiological laboratory of University College, smash up the instruments, liberate the animals and thrash the vivisectors, there would be a public and legitimate demand for a sufficiently protective police force.'

As much was acknowledged by the home secretary's advisers, who, according to cabinet papers, told Gladstone he had no option but to continue providing police protection for the brown dog. In a refreshingly straightforward memo prompted by Magnus's question, Gladstone's legal adviser told him on 3 February 1908 that the brown dog 'seems simply to be a monument which some people like and some dislike, comparable with the statue of Oliver Cromwell by Westminster, which some people would like to deface and which must have the necessary police protection.

'I cannot find that there is any mode of dealing with this monument

The Daily Graphic's illustrated guide to the protest meetings at Battersea

as illegal,' he went on. 'If it were libellous the persons who put it up could be prosecuted for libel, but it probably is not libellous. If it caused crowds to assemble with consequent obstruction to a highway it could be indicted as a public nuisance, but it does not cause them. I think it is clearly not a seditious libel; it does not bring the crown or the law or the administration of justice into contempt.'

In private, Henry was also reconciled to the continued policing of what was a perfectly legal monument. He had already told Gladstone in a memo dated 30 January 1908 that in the absence of any help with policing costs from Battersea council he would have to save money by scaling down the 24-hour cover. As if to justify this reduced attention he added that the memorial 'is certainly not a work of art and cannot be of much value'.

Another Home Office adviser revealed that the Commissioner's letter to Battersea council had, in any case, probably been prompted more out of concern that he should protect himself against legal action than from any real prospect of getting Battersea to contribute to the rising costs. 'There will always be the chance ... that a surprise attack on [the brown dog] might prove successful, and in view of the liability of the police to damages for riot, it might be well for them to address a strong representation to Battersea council as to the provocation caused by the inscription,' he said. 'Such a warning would be useful in meeting a claim for damages if the statue were damaged by riotous students under section 2(1) of the Riot (Damages) Act 1886.'

A month later on 5 March 1908, the council of University College bowed to the inevitable when it decided that no legal action could be taken against Battersea council. The following week, Battersea was handed a petition signed by 1,035 students of the University of London asking the council to remove the words 'University College' from the inscription. The petition, which the college claimed had been signed by some 'strong anti-vivisectionists', said the issue at hand was 'not whether vivisection is right or wrong, but whether it its not highly unjust to single out one college and attack it for doing what the large majority of universities are doing'.

The progressives gave the argument cursory consideration at their next council meeting but decided to take no action, claiming they could not in any case make a change to the fountain without the consent of the donor and guarantor. A motion that Woodward should be approached with the idea was defeated, although councillor William Willis showed the first signs of a potential weakening in the progressive's position when he declared that if the memorial was left alone in the future, the time might come when the council could 'calmly and dispassionately' review the situation.

Some anti-doggers saw this as a sign that the council was preparing to climb down after a suitable interval, ready in the fullness of time that the fountain's inscription had served its purpose by drawing attention to vivisection and was no longer needed. The progressives were, after all, going through a decidedly rough patch as they grappled with a £25,000 overdraft partly created by overspending – and it might have been to their advantage to deflect criticism in other areas. There may also have been a convenient justification for re-wording the inscription, as there had recently been complaints that it had faded to the point where it had become almost unreadable.

Whatever hopes the municipal reformers had were soon dashed, however. Willis was one of the less radical progressives, so his standpoint was hardly representative, and in any case he had qualified his remarks by saying that the right time to remove the memorial would probably be when new anti-vivisection legislation made its presence unnecessary. In May, Runeckles asked if the council was now ready to do anything about the dog, given that ' a sort of half promise' had been made to look at the situation once the furore had died down. He drew a blank.

By the summer of 1908 the general furore had indeed died down. Since receipt of the Commissioner's letter Battersea council had erected two sentry boxes for the use of police guarding the monument, but at a July meeting in Battersea Town Hall councillor Willis told an audience gathered to discuss the public control of hospitals that it was absurd to suppose the fountain still required special police protection. The police were wasting time and energy standing there, and in any case if someone did destroy the dog, a larger and better one would be put in its place, with even more publicity for the anti-vivisectionist cause.

Even if the progressives were willing to change the inscription, what to put in its place? Any new engraving could prove just as controversial. A long-running correspondence between Coleridge and Paget in The Times throughout December 1907 had centred on exactly what an amended fountain might say, yet neither could even come close to agreeing a form of words. Coleridge suggested an new inscription in which he admitted that the brown dog had been anaesthetised, therefore contradicting his evidence at the 1903 trial, but Paget was not impressed and replied with his own version which he said the vivisectionists would be happy to endorse. It read: 'To a dog that was twice anaesthetised for experiments and was killed under the anaesthetic. After the first experiment it was soon quite well and happy; and they kept it, and took care of it, just as the keepers take care of the animals at the Zoological Gardens. It never felt anything during the experiments. It died under anaesthesia, as the dogs die that are not claimed at the Home for Lost Dogs.' Coleridge, needless to say, did not take a fancy to the new version and The Times called a halt to the debate.

Ironically, some of the more militant pro-vivisectionists had decided that the fight to remove the inscription should be abandoned for fear of giving the 'antis' any more publicity. The BMJ, which complained that the dog was 'being used as an advertisement of anti-vivisectionism', urged the students 'to let the Battersea fanatics worship their idol undisturbed'. Now forced to admit that there could be no legal objection to its wording, it continued to maintain that the fountain was 'in the moral sense, a lie, for it insinuates what is false,' but argued that it would be better 'to leave the grotesque effigy alone, for the time must come when the good people of Battersea will be ashamed of the monument of falsehood put up in their midst.'

There appear to have been vague plans within University College to create a 'Brown Dog League' to organise persistent attacks on the memorial throughout 1908, but if anything it was now the anti-vivisectionists who were trying to keep the issue on the boil. In an ironic turnaround, a 26 June debate on vivisection at the Royal Institute of Medicine in Hanover Square had been noisily disrupted by angry supporters of the dog. 'Anti-vivisection is a subject upon which tender hearted people feel so keenly that it is difficult to keep the emotions under strict control,' said a brazen Abolitionist, which had happily condemned the vivisectionists' activities earlier in the year. 'Such expressions as were given were clearly not premeditated like those of medical students ... and may therefore be readily excused.'

The students had tried all they could to rid themselves of the dog – through demonstrations, the disruption of meetings, petitions, legal advice, pressure on the home secretary and council motions. Yet the brown dog supporters had weathered the storm and seemed to be the stronger for it. As 1908 drew to a close the dog's future looked brighter than it had done for some time.

What's more, it had become a confirmed national celebrity, 'a hero of song, ballad and sketch' which had even appeared in the script of a pantomime in Drury Lane. Many a painfully-worded brown dog poem appeared in the newspapers and magazines of the era, re-fitted to the tunes of the day and bringing new meaning to the word 'doggerel'. Though the debate behind it was serious, the brown dog could always raise smiles as well as hackles. Even some of those who wanted the fountain removed had developed a grudging affection for the serene-looking dog standing on top of it.

'He is playing the part which every known martyr, consciously or unconsciously has enacted – that of drawing humanity above the limits of its ordinary moral perception,' said Ford triumphantly that year. 'Everything has been tried ... and yet the dog is victorious.'

all change

turnaround in Battersea ... official moves to remove dog ... a night-time disappearance ... indecision and a legal challenge ... an indistinct death

THE BROWN DOG'S ascendancy was to be short-lived. For the next year it enjoyed one of its quietest spells since the unveiling ceremony in 1906, practising its enigmatic look as life went by on the Latchmere Recreation Ground. But by November 1909 Battersea was to experience a political sea change that altered the face of the recreation ground forever.

The progressives had been in power since the creation of the municipal borough of Battersea in 1900 and for a further five years before that when it was known as the Battersea Vestry. Through a series of alliances of liberals and labourites, they had firmly connected Battersea with radicalism in the public mind, yet the alliance had been showing signs of tension in recent times, not least over the maverick behaviour of MP John Burns, who appeared to be moving ever rightwards and had now taken a cabinet position in the liberal government. Rate rises and spending plans had also put pressure on the progressives, who had come under concerted attack for the past three years over their radical policies and had experienced a partial split by the beginning of November 1909, when they stood once again at the local elections.

By contrast, the municipal reformers were now a more cohesive force standing for lower rates and a business-like approach to running the council, and after 16 years in power the progressives were not expecting an easy ride. Yet the municipal reformers had been through some internal strife of their own and were not talking up their chances. Nobody foresaw the startling result that followed.

The election candidates had barely begun to gather in Battersea Town Hall at 11pm on Monday 1 November 1909 when the first shock result arrived. Willis, by now the progressive mayor, had been defeated. By 1am, as crowds sang and cheered in the streets outside the hall, the town clerk was able to announce the results in full; the progressives had been routed. Only two of their 54 candidates had been elected and the municipal reformers – who won 55 per cent of the votes polled compared to the progressives' 37 per cent – had all but swept the board. Three years earlier the progressives had held 30 seats, six years earlier they had won 38, and in 1900 they had 37; now they had just two, held by Thomas Brogan and Patrick Brolly, in Despard's poverty-stricken stronghold of Nine Elms.

The results were greeted with wild cheering by municipal reformers crowded into Theatre Street at the side of the hall. 'The stronghold of progressive socialism has been stormed and taken, and the inhabitants can breathe freely once more,' wrote a gleeful South Western Star reader. The Wandsworth Borough News rejoiced at the end of '15 years of the most tyrannous monopoly and domination'. Battersea prepared for a new era of conservative politics under its first non-progressive council.

Even the municipal reformers hadn't expected such a staggering victory, although with hindsight a defeat of some sort was predictable. There was bound to have been a substantial backlash against any party that had been in power since before the beginning of the century, but squabbles within the progressive alliance had also weakened its position by prompting some previously supportive groups to leave the all-important Battersea Trades and Labour Council in 1908. That opened the way for break-away socialist and independent labour candidates to split the working class vote in some wards.

Several years of bad press had also successfully propagated a widely-held negative image of a profligate party interested more in attending to eccentric 'side issues' such as the brown dog than concentrating on running the borough efficiently and cheaply. While the progressives still maintained popularity with a strong section of the working class, their increased spending had done little to impress the ratepayers, who could be relied upon to vote in greater relative force when election turnouts were poor, as they tended to be in local polls. Many Battersea ratepayers had proved themselves fairly liberal at previous elections, but had now begun to resent the extra strain on their pockets. The opinion of the borough's female population was largely irrelevant, as although all males over the age of 21 had the vote in 1909, only women paying rates of £12 a year and acting as heads of their households were entitled to take part in the poll.

The change in administration was stark and immediate. When the new members held their first meeting a week after the election, on Tuesday 9 November 1909, seats in the public gallery, which were normally filled by unemployed local men, had been set aside for the fragrant friends of municipal reformist members. The jobless found spaces in the remaining available corners as the new regime filed in. 'As a whole the new members were much better groomed than the old ones used to be,' said the South Western Star pointedly. 'One or two of them appeared in evening dress.'

Ironically, thanks to the County and Borough Councils Act of 1907 which allowed women to stand in local elections, the new council included its first ever woman, the municipal reformist Edie Brown, who was unashamedly stared at by the gallery as she walked in for the meeting. Little business was done at that initial gathering, save for the confirmation of draper John Astill as the municipal reformers' leader and Lancastrian headmaster Peter Haythornthwaite as mayor for the year. But the 'moderates' as they liked to style themselves, had already set the tone for the rest of their administration.

The brown dog memorial had not figured as a direct election issue in 1909, although it had been held up for some time as a prime example of the progressive's 'faddist' excesses. There had been no manifesto promises to get rid of it, nor any meaningful mention of it in electoral debates, from either side. Yet now the municipal reformers were in power the dog began to take on new significance as an unwanted link with the progressive era. If Astill and Haythornthwaite, two of the most vocal critics of the brown dog, could get rid of this symbol of the left-wing past, the reformers would be able to wipe the slate clean – ready for a fresh start where 'common sense' and the ratepayers held sway.

So it was, rather bizarrely, that the brown dog became the single most important policy issue during the new party's first few weeks in power. Egged on by the local and national press, which had immediately challenged the new administration to modify or remove the fountain's controversial inscription, the reformers let it be known that much of their first real business meeting, on 8 December 1909, would be devoted to considering the dog's future.

In part justification for such swift action, they pointed to a strange incident on Monday 8 November, only a week after the election, when a 22-year-old medical student, Arthur Allan, was arrested in Burns Road after trying to bribe a policeman just a few yards from the brown dog.

Allan had sidled up to the police officer, who was guarding the memorial, at around 8.15pm that evening. He asked the time and chatted about the cold weather, then offered the constable £5 if he would walk over to a corner of the recreation ground and turn his back. When the policeman refused, Allan moved up to the brown dog, read the inscription, and told the officer: 'I would like to see that smashed.' He offered further bribes of increasing value until, with the bidding at £15, the policeman decided to arrest him under the Malicious Damage to Property Act.

At South Western Police court the next day, Allan argued that he had no crowbar or hammer on him at the time and that he had only been joking. He had been put up to it by friends and had no serious intention of damaging the memorial. 'I was induced to act as agent on behalf of others to see what could be done about it,' he told the court. 'I'm very sorry I ever had anything to do with it now.' The magistrate concluded that Allan had not been joking and had an 'evil design' on the dog. He was bound over to keep the peace for six months in the sum of 40s.

Conspiracy theorists might argue that Allan and his friends chose a suspiciously convenient time to harass the dog, bringing it once more into the public eye just as the reformers had gained power. After all, Allan's actions allowed those who had opposed the memorial to argue that despite it recent period in the shadows it had lost none of its capacity to incite trouble and create bad publicity. With such a recent example of its continued threat to hand, the new administration now had the perfect excuse for an urgent re-examination of the memorial's future.

There is, though, no evidence to back up such a theory. What is more likely is that Allan and his backers felt the dramatic disappearance of the progressives in Battersea would allow them to destroy the dog with much less resistance. They took the first available opportunity, but came up against an incorruptible policeman.

Whatever the motivation for the Burns Road bribery incident, it certainly allowed the municipal reformers to publicise their new plans for the memorial in the spotlight of renewed national interest. Mayor Haythornthwaite made a point of briefing sympathetic newspapers well in advance of the next council meeting. 'The first idea was to ask for the inscription to be altered,' he told the Daily Mail. 'But we saw that even in that case the statue would still be objectionable to some people and that the better course would be to hand it back to the people who gave it to us.'

As promised, the council spent most of its meeting on Wednesday 8 December 1909 discussing the brown dog, despite protests from some councillors that they were wasting time over an unimportant matter. Most of the debate centred on a recommendation from the council's highways and dustings committee that the borough solicitor should be allowed to arrange for the return of the memorial to the International Anti-Vivisection Council. 'The fountain involves considerable expenditure in the way of police supervision and causes obstruction in what is now practically a public highway,' said the committee's report. 'We do not think that these two points were contemplated when the fountain was erected, and we recommend that the solicitor be instructed to negotiate for its removal and for its return to the donors.'

Councillors agreed to hear a ten-minute presentation from an outside deputation headed by former mayor Bill Rines, who had unveiled the dog at its opening ceremony. Claiming to speak on behalf of the 'citizens of Battersea', Rines argued that the fountain now belonged to the people of the borough, 'who regard the dog as one of their possessions' and did not want it given away.

In any case, he added, no-one had ever really called for the dog itself to be removed, just for a change to the inscription. The reformers should not rush into anything they might regret. Out of power and with the prospect of the dog disappearing altogether, the progressives' hard line had clearly softened. When councillor Henry Bigden asked Rines whether he would be satisfied if the inscription was changed while the dog remained, Rines said he was positive that 'any reasonable suggestion' would be favourably received.

The deputation's pleas seemed to have some effect, for a number of municipal reformers objected to the idea of sending back the memorial, pushing instead for a change to the inscription. One councillor, local GP John Richards, even argued that there should be no inscription at all given that the dog had now served its anti-vivisectionist purpose – a compromise which appeared to get lost in the general rhetoric.

Even within the massed ranks of its own councillors the municipal reform leadership had a hard time sustaining its argument that the dog had suddenly become an obstruction – or that it was adding substantially to the cost of the police rate. Only market traders wheeling their barrows on a short cut through the recreation ground had found any difficulty getting past the fountain, and removing the dog would have cut such a small amount off the total cost of London's policing that it would have made no difference to the police rate. In the end a large majority threw out the highways committee recommendation and voted in favour of an amendment from Leonard McManus, an Irish-born GP and prominent mason, that the highways committee should get to work devising a new, less controversial inscription to replace the existing one. The dozens of anti-vivisectionists packed into the public gallery breathed a partial sigh of relief.

Some observers subsequently accused the rank and file municipal reformers of running scared, that they were afraid that despite their dislike of the monument any decision to return the dog to its owners would spark off disturbances in Battersea. 'There is naturally much resentment in Battersea over the moderate betrayal and it remains to be seen whether the ratepayers there will allow the new council ... to remove a feature of the borough which none but a few riotous medical students dislike,' said the Morning Leader.

Public discussion now switched to what the new inscription might say – and more importantly, whether the International Anti-Vivisection Council would accept the new version. Certainly they were odds-on to reject the suggestion from 'an eminent member of the medical profession' in the Daily Mail that the new wording should finish by saying: 'this dog was free alike from fear and suffering, it died neither of starvation nor of overfeeding, nor of burdens from old age. It just died in its sleep.' But would they accept any tinkering at all? Lind-af-Hageby, who was likely to have some influence on their decision, thought not. 'My strong personal view is that as the memorial was accepted by the Battersea Council in 1906 we should now refuse to take it back and leave the onus of its disposal to the present representatives of Battersea,' she said. Although the Battersea progressives may have been prepared to see the dog tampered with, the anti-vivisectionist movement as a whole appeared to be against the idea.

As the year turned and the highways committee appeared to be discussing a new version of the inscription, organised anti-vivisectionist protest began to gather apace. On Monday 24 January 1910 Willis, Woodward, Rines and a large force of stewards turned up at Battersea Town Hall for a public meeting to argue about the council's plans. There was a modest crowd of 100 which the organisers blamed on bad weather, but police reinforcements had nonetheless been called to guard the memorial after rumours that it would be attacked while the meeting took place.

A dozen students in the audience made their presence known by knocking their sticks on the floor at the back of the hall, but were swiftly surrounded by stewards and remained quiet for the rest of the meeting (save for two short speeches from their representatives) as speaker after speaker supported a motion opposing 'any interference with the brown dog memorial'. Willis, who said there had never been any need 'for half the alarm and certainly not a quarter of the expense' occasioned by the memorial, revealed that a protest petition bearing the signatures of around 20,000 local people had been collected since the council had revealed its plans just over a month previously.

Two days later the massive bundle of papers now bearing 20,615 signatures was formally handed in to a wholly unimpressed mayor Haythornthwaite, who gave it a cursory glance and laid it to one side. Given his plans for the forthcoming council meeting on Wednesday 9

February, the petition was by now a huge irrelevance. Privately he had already decided to shepherd through a new motion that the council should forget about changing the inscription and revert to his original plan of returning the memorial to its donors.

Accordingly, at the 9 February meeting Haythornthwaite disclosed that the highways and dustings committee had noted the McManus motion passed before Christmas, but had decided not to tamper with the inscription and was now repeating its earlier recommendation 'that steps be taken with a view to the removal of the fountain and its return to the donors'. Quite how a lowly sub-committee could blatantly ignore instructions from full council was not made clear, but it soon began to dawn on the brown dog supporters in the public gallery that while everyone had assumed the highways committee had been considering possible compromise inscriptions for the past month, it had in fact been doing nothing of the sort. It had refused to do so, twice deferring any discussion of the matter until deciding on 31 January to ask full council to reconsider its position.

Progressive William Watts, who along with railway clerk Augustus West had been elected to serve on the council as an alderman, was virtually dumb struck and clearly shaken by such 'impudence', much to the amusement of his political foes in the council chamber. His demeanour hardly improved when the town clerk, Marcus Wilkins, revealed that none of the council's officers had even approached the International Anti Vivisection Council about a possible change to the inscription. West also lost his cool, threatening violence against anyone who put their hands on the memorial. 'I shall be very sorry for the people who are engaged in the actual removal because I shall take down some living prototypes of that brown dog and they shall show their teeth if there is a chance,' he raged.

Unlike West and Watts, the municipal reformers appeared to have been well prepared for the news. No-one on the governing side batted an eyelid when they heard that their previous decision, reached by a large majority, had been ignored by a subordinate committee. In fact they appeared to have changed their views completely since that earlier meeting, and were now almost all in favour of removing the fountain rather than changing its inscription. While the highways committee had been doing its best to ignore their previous instructions, the municipal reform party whips appeared to have been working hard to change their colleagues' minds – and to instill some party discipline.

The rank and file municipal reformers certainly appeared to have a new-found enthusiasm for ridding the recreation ground of its memorial.

John Eyre, a local artist, said the dog 'was artistically the worst thing I ever saw,' an eyesore which kept police out in the wind and rain; millwright William Scott warned councillors they would look 'an extraordinary set of fools' if they kept a statue which was cursed by the police 'to the fullest extent' and which he estimated was worth about £2 as scrap. McManus said the 20,000-signature petition was 'bogus', probably signed by as many 'babes and sucklings' as adults living in the borough.

Only councillors Brogan and Brolly continued to call for a change to the inscription, arguing that removal of the brown dog would re-advertise the anti-vivisectionist cause and make Battersea a laughing stock. When the final vote came, 41 were in favour of sending the fountain back, only four against.

Such a dramatic turn of events caught the anti-vivisectionists on the hop. Since the pre-Christmas council meeting they had been gearing themselves up to campaign against a newly-worded inscription, but were now facing the imminent removal of the fountain. Luckily for them the council's decision was followed by a curious period of inaction as the Municipal Reform leadership, having now got permission to send the memorial back, tried to decide on the best way forward. 'No-one seems to know exactly what ought to be done next,' said the South Western Star. 'It looks as though some superstitious awe is attached to the brown dog.'

The Municipal Reform leadership's problem was that it was now obliged to inform the International Anti-Vivisection Council that it was returning the memorial, thus opening up the possibility that the donors would refuse to have it back. Faced with such a prospect, some Municipal Reform councillors had begun to have second thoughts about the wisdom of their latest decision, and were becoming increasingly nervous that the council could be drawn into a protracted dialogue accompanied by public unrest. The South Western Star warned the waverers that 'unless they wish to render themselves supremely ridiculous in the eyes of the country – for all the kingdom has heard about the brown dog – they must do away with it, and soon'. If the International Anti-Vivisection Council refused to have its dog back, Battersea 'must shovel it to the side of the road and leave it there to be dealt with by the police as an obstruction'.

In the meantime, public protest had indeed begun to grow. Friends of the brown dog held a well-attended Monday evening meeting at Latchmere Baths on 21 February 1910, supported by anti-vivisectionists from all over the country plus a delegation from France. Councillor West, as if to back up his earlier threats in the council chamber, brought with him a large angry bulldog which, according to one account, 'seemed annoyed by the applause which greeted his appearance on the platform'. All the major anti-vivisectionist figures were there to endorse a resolution that the meeting 'emphatically protests against the decision to remove the brown dog memorial and considers such an action an undesirable concession to organised violence'.

Lind-af-Hageby asked the crowd whether there would have been any establishment outcry if police had been called in to protect the Jenner statue in Kensington Gardens from regular attacks by anti-vaccine demonstrators. Despard appealed for unity in the anti-vivisection movement, which had again been beset by squabbling over the merits of gradualism or total abolition. And John Archer boldly predicted that if the fountain were removed, another site would be found for it in Battersea – where it would stay for two and a half years until the progressives regained power and returned it to Latchmere. The most rousing speech of the night, though, came from the chair, Liberal MP for Exeter and NAVS vice president Sir George Kekewich. 'People of Battersea, see to it that the brown dog is not removed,' he said. 'See to it that you keep up the great reputation of the borough for humanity.'

By now the council had begun to talk to Louisa Woodward about returning the fountain, but had reached an impasse. As expected she appeared to be refusing to accept its return. At a council meeting on 9 March 1910, town clerk Wilkins read out a letter from Woodward's solicitors which claimed she was perfectly satisfied with the current arrangements and saw no reason to remove the fountain. If, however, it was blocking the highway, then she was prepared to agree to the dog's removal from the pathway with a view to re-erecting it a few yards behind the protection of the recreation ground's iron fence – thus also doing away with the need for a day and night guard.

Borough solicitor Paul Caudwell reported that he had met Woodward's representatives to try to hammer out an amicable arrangement, with no success. The council had not been prepared to re-site the dog behind the fence, nor had Woodward liked the council's idea that it should be repositioned in the grounds of the Anti-Vivisection Hospital. In the final analysis, though, Woodward and the council were engaging in fruitless discussion, for by refusing to take the fountain back Woodward had relinquished any say in its future. As long as the dog remained an unwanted gift which the donor would not have back, then the council was within its rights to do whatever it wanted.

Astill therefore moved that the council should now remove the statue without further reference to Woodward's society, and with little debate the motion was carried by 42 votes to four. 'The whole thing was done so quickly that the defenders of the brown dog could hardly realise it,' said the South Western Star. 'The gallery was temporarily paralysed.' Once again the anti-vivisectionists had been overtaken by the pace of the council's decision-making. Having just geared their campaign to resisting the memorial's return to Woodward, they were now facing its disappearance altogether. As they pondered their next move, however, the Municipal Reform leadership was preparing for some night-time activity. When Battersea woke up the next morning the dog had vanished.

'People who take a short cut through the Latchmere Recreation Ground stopped and rubbed their eyes,' said the South Western Star. 'Many stopped so long that they got late to work. The neighbourhood did not seem itself. "What's happened?" people asked each other. Then they noticed a patch of new tar-paving that covered the spot on which the brown dog had stood.' Many locals simply could not believe the dog had gone; some were so convinced it couldn't be true that they refused even to go and see for themselves. Few believed that the council could have acted so swiftly after the previous night's meeting, and the rumour spread that students had taken the dog down in triumph.

The council raid on the dog in the early morning of Thursday 10 March 1910 was so secret that it remains difficult to establish the exact details of what happened, but it was definitely not the work of students. Some sensationalist modern accounts have claimed that between 50 and 120 policemen supervised the destruction at dead of night for fear of a local rebellion, but the job appears to have been carried out by no more than half-a-dozen hand-picked men supervised by the borough surveyor and watched over by a couple of constables.

It was a slick, carefully thought-out operation that must have been planned several days before the council's vote. With a portable derrick and other lifting apparatus, the gang of council workers arrived at the recreation ground in the small hours, showing their credentials to the policemen guarding the memorial and disconnecting the wires of the electric alarm bell before they got to work. They cut off the water supply to the fountain, then swung the derrick into action and lifted the whole monument on to a waiting lorry. Whispering to themselves as they worked, they left shortly before 5am, the dog covered with a tarpaulin as it was driven down Battersea Park Road to a secret destination. Total cost of the night's work was £3 10s 0d.

Only a handful of people were privy to the operation, and the dog's temporary resting place was kept quiet. Some speculated that it had been

Dog gone: police guard the empty spot where the memorial once stood

broken apart and fed into the local 'dust destructor', other accounts maintained it had been taken to the municipal stoneyard, although in fact it had been taken for temporary storage in a bicycle shed at the house of the borough surveyor. Though speculation as to its whereabouts was rife, many were just happy that it had gone. 'We do not deplore its loss,' admitted the South Western Star the following day. 'On the contrary, we admire the promptness and the prudence which for once have distinguished the Battersea Borough Council. We admire the neatness, completeness and the secrecy with which the deed was done.'

The reaction of the Battersea public was less favourable. Once the shock had subsided, several hundred people gathered near the Prince's Head pub about half a mile from the recreation ground on the corner of York Road and Falcon Road, where the usual posse of speakers denounced what one hastily-constructed banner called the 'Midnight abduction of the Brown Dog.' The police guard had remained at the recreation ground despite the dog's absence, and had prevented an impromptu demonstration on the spot where the fountain had been standing 24 hours earlier. There were crowds of jeering spectators in the public gallery at the town hall that night, as councillor Watts tried vainly to elicit more information about the previous night's clandestine activities during a meeting of the normally subdued parliamentary committee. The mayor threatened to have the place cleared out.

Public reaction may have been swift, but confusion reigned among the anti-vivisectionists, who had not been expecting the dog to disappear in such dramatic or secretive circumstances. On the Thursday morning, a few hours after the fountain's removal, Woodward decided on the strange move of seeking a High Court injunction to stop the council taking away the dog – even though it had already done so. Unless Woodward's application was a panic move it is possible that she hadn't yet heard about the dog's removal – and that her court visit was a pre-planned response to the council's Wednesday evening vote. Certainly the judge in charge of the case, Justice Neville, was unaware of the morning's events, and no-one had bothered to tell him that the dog had already been removed when he granted an interim injunction. By the following day he had read the newspapers and had no choice but to reverse his decision. After lengthy discussions Neville then gave Woodward permission to seek a court ruling for the repositioning of the memorial, plus damages. In the meantime, the council agreed to keep the dog in good order in case it had to be put back on its spot. 'Some people supposed that (the dog's removal) would terminate a long and stormy controversy,' said a weary Local Government Chronicle, 'yet it is likely to be the cause of further trouble and anxiety to all the parties concerned'.

As the dog languished in its hiding place and the legal wheels ground ahead slowly, somewhere between 1,000 and 3,000 people assembled in Hyde Park on the Saturday afternoon of 18 March 1910 for a protest walk to Trafalgar Square. At the head of the throng was a real-life double of the brown dog sitting in a specially decorated car next to a human demonstrator and a large placard reading: 'Why should we be vivisected?' When the demonstrators reached Trafalgar Square, Sir George Kekewich said Battersea council had acted in cowardly fashion by making its move against the dog under cover of darkness 'for fear that the honest working men of Battersea would have seen that it stayed in its place'. The Crown Princess of Germany had taken an interest in the matter, he said, and there were hopes of involving the royal family in Britain too. Lind-af-Hageby promised that a new memorial would be erected if the old one was destroyed, 'to show our hatred of a system which is not only barbarous but also unscientific and misleading'.

The High Court action against the council was not destined to give the anti-vivisectionists immediate satisfaction. Although Woodward had been granted leave to bring her case, legal preparations were to take the

all change

Fightback: thousands protest at Trafalgar Square against the dog's removal

best part of nine months – and for the whole of that time the centre of the recreation ground remained bare. As far as the new council was concerned, the battle had already been won.

Now that the much-hated symbol of the progressive era had been dealt with, the municipal reformers felt free to busy themselves with a wholesale reversal of their predecessors' policies in other areas. In April 1910 they announced plans for a series of fierce cutbacks which would mean job losses for dozens of council employees, increased hours for council workers and wage cuts across the board, prompting a union delegation to ask the council 'for heaven's sake to have some consideration for the wives and families of the men who will have the bread taken out of their mouths'. A fund was set up to buy a flagpole so the union flag could be flown at the town hall, and in September 1910 the Anti-Vivisection Hospital's annual carnival had to be cancelled after the council refused to continue its long-standing support for the event. There was even talk of selling off the 'troublesome' Latchmere Estate.

At 10.30am on 20 January 1911, Woodward's High Court action

finally came up for consideration. With Justice Neville again presiding, Woodward's counsel asked the court to order Battersea to restore the fountain to the Latchmere Estate on the grounds that its removal had been contrary to the original agreement made between herself and the council. The International Anti-Vivisection Council would have been quite happy to have changed the inscription to delete any mention of University College, even though it was not libellous, she said – yet Battersea council had never put that proposition to her. Woodward had sent the council leadership a telegram warning that councillors acted 'at their peril' if they took down the fountain, but they had gone ahead anyway.

With Woodward's opening defence completed, Neville stepped in to call a halt to the proceedings. There was no need to take the case any further, he told the court, because he had already decided it must fall. As Woodward's argument rested solely on her claim that an agreement had been made to keep and maintain the fountain, there was no point in proceeding. It was clear to him that there had been no such agreement. The deed of indemnity signed three days before the opening ceremony in 1906 did not mention maintenance, nor did it even represent a contract. 'To my mind there was no contract on the part of the defendants to maintain the fountain accepted by them from the Anti-Vivisection Council,' he said.

Even if he had got so far as to hearing the case in full, said Neville, it was unlikely he would have disagreed with Battersea's proposed defence that the inscription was libellous and defamatory. 'It is clear from the words of the inscription that it is not a mere statement as to the dogs which had suffered in the supposed interests of humanity,' he said. 'On the best construction I can put upon it and on its clear and natural construction it seems to me to be calculated to hold up the University College to public execration and to inflame the public mind against it; and to be calculated to lead to a breach of the peace'. As such he would not have felt able to force the council to keep the brown dog, even if a valid maintenance contract had been made.

On the other hand he sympathised with Woodward's plight, which had been brought about by a wholesale change of administration and 'fluctuation of opinion' at the borough council, causing her 'considerable hardship'. In light of that, he would not force her to pay Battersea council's costs, but he had no power to make any ruling on what should now happen to the memorial – nor what should become of the £300 indemnity. That was a matter for the council to decide. The home secretary of the time, Winston Churchill, sent a representative to observe the court proceedings. In cabinet notes the informant recorded that Justice Neville had brought 'a satisfactory end to this matter'.

Although the case was equally satisfactory for the municipal reformers, it had cost them £108 17s 6d in legal fees, vastly more than the progressives had ever spent on the dog up to that point, and a source of potential embarrassment for an administration which had claimed the memorial's removal would save money.

Further legal costs ensued as Woodward moved to get her £300 and the dog back. On the same day as her defeat in the High Court her solicitors fired off a letter demanding return of the memorial, plus the money, with almost five years' worth of interest. When councillors finally got round to considering her demand at full council on 8 March 1911, they voted 40 to 14 in favour of destroying the dog and refusing to return the £300. Astill said they would melt down the bronze and smash up the inscription, but would keep the fountain for use elsewhere. The indemnity money would have to remain in the council's bank account until the possibility of legal action had subsided. A motion that the dog should be sent to the Battersea museum was defeated.

A small pocket of municipal reformers were upset by the decision: Henry Bigden accused his colleagues of plotting 'an act of vandalism' which would render the council 'worse than the medical students', and Edie Brown thought the idea a 'childish gesture'. The progressives were once again apoplectic. West said the vote showed the municipal reformers at their 'vindictive and vicious' worst. 'Did you ever hear anything like it in your life?' he asked. 'Even supposing you went as far as destroying the inscription, what satisfaction can you get out of setting a man with a hammer to smash up the dog?. The reformers were determined to get rid of the memorial altogether because they feared it would be resurrected when the progressives got back into power, he said. 'The moderate party knows we shall come back with a majority and shall have that dog back again. The men who are responsible for the robbery ought to be absolutely ashamed of themselves.' Keeping the dog and the money amounted to theft, he added.

The hardliners were unmoved. William Manser argued that the dog was now the property of the council, which had the perfect right to do with it as it wished. Councillor William Evans, a schoolteacher, suggested it should be melted down and made into a chain for the mayor, a badge of office which the progressives had scorned but which the new administration had now committed itself to buy. Another colleague said it should be put into the dust destructor 'where it should be sent to oblivion'.

The decision having been made, the council again acted swiftly. Within a week the Wandsworth Borough News was reporting that 'naught but a shapeless heap remains for the memory of the little quadruped who once caused such a commotion'. Details of its death were hazy, although the South Western Star claimed to have information that the bronze part of the monument had been 'smashed almost to atoms' by a local blacksmith 'who was as relentless as any vivisectionist'.

'He spat on his horny hands, raised his heavy hammer aloft and brought it down with a tremendous force on the back of the poor little brown dog' it said in what appears to be an account drawn more from the imagination than hard fact. 'Blow after blow was delivered, then the fragments were collected, placed in a sack and sealed.' The value of the broken metal was put at 3s 'or 30 pieces of silver – a fitting sum', but it seems the metal was probably not sold, just melted in the council's dust destructor furnaces. The Times said merely that 'the fragments have been disposed of'.

What happened to the rest of the memorial is even less clear, although newspapers reported that the marbled inscription was cut away from the granite base on 23 March 1911 and almost certainly destroyed. A precise date of death is impossible to pinpoint, but that day – nine years and three weeks after the original brown dog was killed – is as good as any. The monument itself had survived around four and a half years, probably longer than the real life animal it was based on, though not by much.

A meeting of the highways and dustings committee on 13 March 1911 was supposed to have considered a site for what remained of the memorial – namely the trough and fountain. Yet its members adjourned without coming to a conclusion, and do not appear to have considered the issue again. In all probability the last surviving section of the troublesome memorial was dumped quietly during the next couple of weeks for fear that even a small fragment of the original could have served as a rallying point for anti-vivisectionists. 'This much is for certain,' said the South Western Star, 'if any alleged relics of the brown dog are ever hawked about for sale, the public may be sure they will be spurious.'

The council had confirmed under progressive questioning that it had finally destroyed the memorial, yet the last movements of the brown dog are sufficiently hazy to cast doubt over what really happened during its dying days. Just over a year had passed from the night it was taken down to the point when it was supposedly destroyed, yet during that time there were no positive sightings of the dog, nor was there any serious information as to its whereabouts. Given the extraordinary interest in its fate one might have expected someone, somewhere, to have found out exactly where the memorial was lying.

The original dismantling operation had been well planned and secretive, but to keep the lid on the monument's position for a further 12 months must have been a difficult task. Marjorie Martin, the borough surveyor's daughter, claimed in 1956 that the dog had been moved from her father's bicycle shed to a 'corporation yard', but if the dog had been kept in a council shed for such a lengthy period then surely some council workers would have got wind of its whereabouts – and it's unlikely they would have been able to keep the news to themselves. It is not impossible, therefore, that the memorial may have been destroyed far earlier than the council let on.

Certainly the newspapers at the time were unsure whether it had been destroyed or merely kept to one side, and the Municipal Reform leaders pointedly refused to discuss its movements. At the March 1911 meeting which finally decided the dog's fate, councillor William Evans had suggested various fates for the dog 'if it has not already been destroyed.' Why should he add such a rider? Did Evans and his backbench Municipal Reform colleagues suspect that their leadership had killed the dog off much earlier?

It's a possibility with only circumstantial supporting evidence, yet it would make sense of the sometimes confusing turn of events after the dog was taken away from Latchmere Recreation Ground. It would explain, for instance, why the council, having originally tried to return the dog to Woodward, then decided to destroy it as soon as her solicitors asked for it back. If the dog no longer existed, the municipal reform leadership would not have been able to return it; hence the immediate need to vote for its 'destruction'. Likewise it would explain the failure of the highways and dustings committee to find a new position for the trough and fountain: if the bottom part of the monument no longer existed, then the committee could not have moved it.

If Astill and Haythornthwaite really did sanction the dog's destruction at some point after the night of 10 March 1910, then they would have been treading a tightrope for the whole of the following year – not least by breaking their assurance to the high court that they would keep it. It would certainly have been a dangerous path to tread, and one which they are unlikely to have taken. But the possibility that they did so remains.

Whatever the timing of the dog's destruction, the local newspapers, having campaigned against the dog for so long, actually appeared to have some pangs of regret at its departure. 'I am afraid only that Battersea will be a duller place now that little Fido has passed the terrible fires of eternal oblivion,' said a Wandsworth Borough News columnist. 'Ah me for the days of riot and glorious excitement.'

In fact the paper, which had only wanted a changed inscription not total demolition, condemned its destruction as a 'childish' and 'illogical' move. 'If it was wrong for the progressive council to accept it, then it is still wrong of the moderate council to injure it in any way,' it argued. 'By taking the impatient course of destroying the statue, the council will find that the dear little animal will experience a sort of resurrection in the minds of the tender hearted.'

For the anti-vivisectionists, and Woodward in particular, there was little to be done except grieve for one of the most controversial statues ever erected in Britain – and to think about legal action for return of the International Anti-Vivisection Council's £300. In May 1911, before the matter could get to court, Battersea wrote a letter to Woodward informing her that as long as no libel in connection with the memorial was taken in the interim her £300 plus interest would be returned on 3 July 1911. On that day the money was delivered, and the last physical Battersea connection with the dog was severed.

For The Lancet, the move brought an end to a monument which 'was erected in prejudice [and] has at last been overcome by considerations of common sense'. For Bayliss's son Leonard, the whole affair had exposed 'the emotional, unreasoning and often highly unscrupulous methods used by many of the opponents of experiments on animals ... and alienated many who had previously sympathised with the anti-vivisectionist cause'.

For others, the handling of the brown dog affair continued to rankle. In November 1911, as one of the dog's greatest tormentors, Arthur Runeckles, was installed as Battersea's new mayor, the progressives refused to support the customary vote of thanks to his predecessor, Peter Haythornthwaite, who had been one of the slipperiest movers during the hectic few weeks that led to the monument's disappearance.

During the key weeks after the Christmas of 1910, when the Municipal Reform leadership had gradually begun to realise that part measures would fail to dampen the controversy which habitually surrounded the memorial, Haythornthwaite and Astill had managed to steer the council from its stated policy of changing the memorial's inscription to sending it back and then to destroying it altogether.

To the dog's supporters their scheming was outrageous, but to the municipal reformers it was essential. Any other course of action would have preserved the bronze animal's spirit and nourished its cause. A changed or nullified inscription would still have left the monument in place as a focal point for anti-vivisectionists, its return to the donors would have allowed it to be re-sited within the borough on private land with more publicity, and if it had reappeared in a museum it would have been visited by thousands as its story grew into legend. Consignment to the dust destructor gave the dog some of the most sympathetic coverage of its short life, although only for a few weeks. If it had been allowed to stay – in whatever form – then its fame would have guaranteed future controversy. Those in favour of vivisection had no choice but to kill it off.

reborn

life after the dog ... an assessment of its significance ... the class war ... renewed interest 70 years later... a modern day successor

THE DECISION TO destroy the brown dog memorial was a sound one as far as supporters of vivisection were concerned. Within a month of its destruction there was nothing left for the newspapers to write about — and after a year it was already a forgotten piece of history.

Had the International Anti-Vivisection Council moved swiftly enough to retain it in some form, then the dog could have had a life for it elsewhere, perhaps returning to the borough when the political climate was more conducive. But with no remnants of the memorial left, the onus was on the anti-vivisectionists to create another monument and to find willing recipients elsewhere – unlikely given the turbulent history of the brown dog in Battersea. The progressives had promised to bring the fountain back to Latchmere once they regained power, yet now it was gone they could not make good their pledge. In any case, the 1909 election defeat had hit the progressives hard, and when they did get back into power in 1912 many of the old supporters of the dog had disappeared into the background. A smaller, more functional drinking fountain with no anti-vivisectionist connections eventually appeared in the brown dog's place, although it was taken down during the Second World War and failed to reappear in peacetime. The Anti-Vivisection Hospital and the dogs' home remained, but the borough's clear links with anti-vivisectionism swiftly began to weaken. Except for an occasional retrospective newspaper article, the brown dog memorial wallowed in obscurity for the next 70 years.

For the various key figures who outlived the dog there were plenty of other things to occupy the mind. William Bayliss, the small, quiet man who had first sparked off the affair with his libel suit against Coleridge, went from strength to strength at University College, where he was raised to the professorship of general physiology a year after the memorial's demise. Two years later he wrote *Principles of General philosophy*, a standard textbook which became a classic of its kind and was hailed by The Times as 'one of the most remarkable scientific books ever written'.

In the early 1920s he again became entangled in vivisectionist controversy when it was revealed that stolen dogs had been used at University College for experimentation, but he was knighted in 1922, two years before his death in Hampstead at age 64. Henry Dale, the young student who finally killed the brown dog in 1903, eventually became Sir Henry Dale, a well known and respected physiologist who won a Nobel Prize in 1936 and chaired the Wellcome Trust for 22 years up to 1960. He died at Cambridge in 1968.

The students' leader Howard Lister went on to greater things, too, displaying legendary bravery as a medical man in the trenches during the First World War. As Captain Lister he won the Military Cross in 1915, later adorning it with two bars for leading his stretcher bearers under constant fire, and was twice mentioned in dispatches. Further outstanding bravery won him a DSO in December 1917, shortly before he was forced home with gas poisoning and bronchitis. He went back to the front and was killed in 1918 by a trench mortar bomb in Asiago, Italy, aged 32.

Those who knew Lister claimed his student adventures with the brown dog had provided a valuable trial run for the leadership skills he later exhibited in war. 'He was in all the demonstrations the moving spirit and held the whole body of his followers in control,' said his biographer William Seton. 'This was the first public exhibition of the powers of leadership which he possessed to an unusually high degree. He became known by name and by face to most of the medical students of London of his time, and in the years of the war many of them were wont to claim acquaintance with him in messes and on the battlefield.' The University College roll of honour says the brown dog affair 'showed Lister's powers and marked him out for leadership'; certainly it is possible the entire controversy would have faded but for his lively intervention.

For Lister's vegetarian arch enemy, Louise Lind-af-Hageby, the brown dog affair was a useful training ground too, establishing her as a familiar, charismatic figure in English society and honing her talents as a prominent speaker and campaigner. 'Slight and vivid with clear blue eyes and a mass of brown hair, she radiates that subtle impelling force that makes her a charming friend and a deadly enemy,' said the Star, which described her as 'an orator with few equals in this country'.

Lind-af-Hageby retained a faint but distinctive Swedish accent and maintained her contacts with her native country, as well as a chalet near Chamonix in France, but from the first stirrings of the brown dog affair, Britain had become her home. As the controversy rumbled on in 1909, she set up her own British-based organisation, the Animal Defence and Anti-Vivisection Society, which she used to continue her life-long battle against animal experiments.

She was a figure on the world stage too, organising an international anti-vivisection congress with Louisa Woodward in London in July 1909, which was soured by the emergence of a rival convention set up by the World League Against Vivisection, a strictly abolitionist group which objected to her gradualist approach. She fell victim to a propaganda campaign by the outright abolitionists, but her event in Caxton Hall was still the more successful, attended by 250 societies from 30 countries.

Lind-af-Hageby's campaigning life was not confined to animal rights, however. She also nurtured an interest in female emancipation and world peace, and many years after the publication of *The Shambles of Science* she wrote other passionate and controversial books, such as *Unbounded Gratitude!* a 1920 tome on a woman's right to work, and four years later, *Be Peacemakers*, 'an appeal to women of the 20th century to remove the causes of war'. She also chronicled the life of the Swedish playwright August Strindberg.

Her family wealth allowed her to live the busy but untroubled life of a gentlewoman, attending to her various causes and controversies. She also used her money for charitable purposes, working on the continent to help house children from destitute families. Throughout her life she never ducked a challenge, and was involved in another prominent libel case in April 1913, this time as the plaintiff, after the Pall Mall Gazette accused the Animal Defence and Anti-Vivisection Society of carrying out 'a systematic campaign of falsehood'.

At issue was her society's dramatic shop window display in Sloane Street, which featured a model of a mongrel strapped up for vivisection, just as the brown dog had been. Lind-af-Hageby argued that the Gazette's derogatory comments were clearly directed at her personally, but she was on weak ground, for the article had not mentioned her by name. Although the Daily Telegraph, of all papers, praised her for her 'high standard of intellectual ability', the jury ruled in favour of the Gazette's wealthy proprietor, William Astor, and she had to pay costs of £6,561. As in the Bayliss v Coleridge case, the Daily News launched a fund, raising £6,000 towards her final bill.

The defeat did not dim her spirit, though, and she continued to speak all around the world for many years, putting across her ideas until well into her sixties. In 1931 she revisited Paris to draw up a progress

In later life: Lister and Lind-af-Hageby

report on the Pasteur Institute which had first prompted her crusade, and in 1948 she was still spritely enough to join a deputation to the home secretary Chuter Ede asking for a national inquiry into animal experiments. She died, aged 83, in 1963.

Stephen Coleridge continued as honorary secretary of the NAVS until his death in 1936 and, like Lind-af-Hageby, also produced a number of books, including *The Idolatry of Science* and *Vivisection*. But his great joy was poetry, and he also wrote some rather self-indulgent volumes such as *Letters to My Grandson on the Glory of English Poetry* and *A Morning in My Library*. He was an accomplished amateur painter who was shown at various exhibitions.

For the three humble local councillors most associated with the brown dog, life centred on more mundane activities. Bill Rines, who as mayor had presided over the unveiling of the dog and had remained one of its most consistent supporters, devoted most of the rest of his life to teaching and trade union activities, and died in 1925 of cancer. William Watts, who had steered through the original application to put up the fountain and had remained to fight the dog's corner while swamped by municipal reformers in 1909, became a justice of the peace in 1917 and spent a quiet life out of politics until his death in 1932. Augustus West, who took the destruction of the dog to heart more than anyone else, became a London County councillor for Battersea in 1913. He showed more political ambition than his colleagues, standing five times for Parliament as a liberal or independent liberal, each time unsuccessfully and lastly in Battersea at the age of 60. He retired to Woodmansterne in Surrey in 1940 and died three years later.

The dog's more middle class conservative opponents took a more prominent place in local life. Arthur Runeckles continued as a councillor while working as principal of the Educational Correspondence College until he was appointed as a justice of the peace in 1928. But his greatest sphere of influence was in the masonic world, where as a leading freemason he became the worshipful master of the Duke of Fife Lodge in 1925. He died in 1944.

Organisationally, the progressives spent three years in some disarray until winning power back at the 1912 elections before a final split during the First World War. The Labour Party won control in 1919 and the municipal reformers had to resign themselves to a further lengthy spell as Battersea's natural opposition, eventually dropping their 'non-political' pretence to stand as Conservatives.

On the local scene, the memorial became little more than a good story which symbolised the heartfelt but sometimes slapstick rift between the progressives and the municipal reformers. Yet for British anti-vivisectionists the brown dog was one of the most significant rallying points of this century, contributing to the rapid growth in opposition to animal experiments during the Edwardian period and, crucially, moving the debate on vivisection out of its middle and upper class arena and into the public domain.

For once, the brown dog memorial had allowed ordinary people to talk about the real life case of a real life animal, and a dog – man's best friend – at that. As the BMJ pointed out prior to the 1903 libel trial, Coleridge had homed in on the plight of a little brown terrier 'with great judgement, for nearly all Englishmen are lovers of dogs'. To commemorate the dog in bronze was an even more inspired stroke, for here it was brought back to life as an object of affection and respect, serving humans with its fountain while looking out reproachfully at those who chose to experiment on its colleagues. To Edward Ford, the monument used 'a subtle symbology' which led humans and dogs 'peacefully and unitedly to the waters of life ... among which the vivisector's knife would, in their view, sadly rust'.

Dogs, unlike rabbits, rats or guinea pigs, could not easily be joked about. The monument's opponents were forever having to preface their criticisms of the memorial with assurances that they too kept dogs of their own and that, as Councillor McManus said before voting to destroy the memorial, they would 'sooner, in the heat of passion, kill a man than hurt a dog'. So it was that even those who opposed what they saw as the monument's libellous inscription found it difficult not to speak of the bronze dog itself in vaguely affectionate terms: even the South Western Star habitually talked of the 'little brown dog in Battersea'.

For the anti-vivisectionists the memorial was a window of opportunity which they exploited to the full. Although the big-name newspapers were largely against them, they won sympathy over the brown dog from a wide cross-section of the press, and have rarely since been able to generate so much sustained general interest in a single anti-vivisectionist issue.

More tangible benefits were few; the brown dog did not bring forth any changes in the law on vivisection, nor did it seriously undermine establishment support for animal experiments. Yet it did raise the debate to new levels and the controversy over the Bayliss v Coleridge trial did help to generate the climate for the creation of a second royal commission on vivisection, set up in September 1906. The commission's deliberations were tortuous, and the final report – which didn't appear until six years later in 1912 – concluded that no further legislation was necessary. But it did help the anti-vivisectionists keep their campaign on the boil and it gave many of those involved in the brown dog affair, including Woodward, Lind-af-Hageby and Coleridge, the chance to complain that controls on animal experiments had been made worthless by the secrecy surrounding inspections. As a consequence it also ushered in some tightening up of the regulatory system. 'It did not draw aside the curtains of secrecy, but like the brown dog trial, it parted them a little,' said the leading American doctor and anti-vivisectionist Albert Leffingwell.

After the First World War, anti-vivisectionists found it harder to rekindle the interest in their campaigning. The brown dog affair had been more than a national *cause célèbre* in Edwardian Britain – it had helped to keep the schism between abolitionists and gradualists at bay. With the dog gone, the schism was to bedevil the movement for years to come.

For supporters of vivisection, the brown dog affair was an episode they could have done without, but it was not entirely unwelcome – they did after all win the Bayliss v Coleridge libel suit, and in the end they managed to have the memorial destroyed. The antics of the medical students during 1907 and 1908 did little to help them foster an image as reasoned individuals who dealt in logic rather than emotion, but in the process the supporters of vivisection were forced to improve their rusty publicity machine, forming the Medical Research Defence Society in 1908 and mobilising sympathetic sections of the press in their defence. By the end of the controversy it was the anti-vivisectionists, not their opponents, who were out on the streets protesting – a state of affairs which the vivisectionists were much more accustomed to.

The brown dog was, then, an important icon in the history of the arguments between anti-vivisectionists and animal experimenters. But for many it has had a much wider additional significance as a radical symbol adopted by suffragettes, trade unionists and the working class populace of Battersea as a defiant gesture against the ruling elite. It may have begun life as an anti-vivisectionist monument but it certainly did not remain so.

The link between the women's movement and the memorial was particularly strong. Lind-af-Hageby was a keen supporter of votes for women, as was Charlotte Despard and many of the foot soldiers of the anti-vivisectionist movement, who believed that women's suffrage and anti-vivisection were part of the same battle. There is no doubt that women were the prime movers in the myriad anti-vivisection societies of the Edwardian era, and as a consequence were key figures in the brown dog affair. 'At the present moment it seems to me that the greater proportion of those who wholeheartedly and without remuneration give their services to the cause of anti-vivisection are women,' said Ford in 1908. 'There is therefore every reason to anticipate that political freedom for women will mean moral and legal restraint for vivisectors.'

If by political freedom he meant the vote, then he was wrong, although he was not the only one to believe that the causes of anti-vivisection and female emancipation were inextricably linked. Brown dog supporter Sir George Kekewich told a meeting of the Incorporated Parliamentary Association for the Abolition of Vivisection in 1910 that he was 'quite sure that if women have the vote there will be no vivisection' – and the Rev Arthur Mursell, who had been one of the dignitaries at the opening of the memorial, told a 1907 meeting of the NAVS that if suffragettes were on the side of anti-vivisection he would put every other prejudice behind him 'and send them to Parliament to legislate for the cats and dogs'. Even the BMJ warned that 'the welfare of men would have to give way to the comfort of animals if the suffragettes prevail'.

There were actually few, if any, instances of female brown dog supporters publicly and specifically linking the cause of the dog to votes for women, but there is no doubt that many suffragettes saw the dog as a useful rallying point. After all, the core support for Edwardian anti-vivisectionism came from middle class women – and it was they who also provided the backbone of the suffragette movement. It would have been surprising had the two not become intertwined.

Middle class men did not seem to be attracted to the dog's cause in the same numbers, and when the women didn't turn up – as in the first meeting at Battersea Town Hall in 1908 – the show of support was often poor. At the 1903 St James's Hall gathering where Coleridge first spoke of the brown dog, the majority of the audience was female, and most meetings in support of the monument continued to be so throughout the affair. It was women who were to the forefront of the meetings in 1907 and 1908 (although hundreds of working class men showed their support by acting as stewards), and it was women who most often spoke out in the dog's favour on public platforms. Not all of them were supporters of the suffragettes, but the two issues became linked in the public mind.

Although trade unionists were by no means all in favour of women's suffrage, or particularly associated with anti-vivisection, they also proved to be consistent supporters of the brown dog throughout its troubled existence – from the supportive telegrams of outfits such as the Battersea branch of the Operative Bricklayers Society to the constant backing of the Battersea Trades and Labour Council. They were buttressed by broad support from a cross-section of socialists, radicals, home rulers and liberals who chose to see the dog as a focus of Britain's emerging class politics – on the one side a humble monument in one of London's poorest boroughs, on the other the rich, upper class medical students of Gower Street with their Oxbridge connections and their links to conservatism. Lord Llangattock, president of NAVS, was being optimistic when he told the St James's Hall meeting of 1903 that he believed the society had 'at its back the vast majority of the working classes of the country', but he would later have been impressed by the working class interest eventually shown in the plight of the brown dog.

Certainly the people who lived in the area surrounding the monument seem to have adopted the brown dog almost immediately as a symbol of their everyday struggles against authority. The middle class pursuit of anti-vivisectionism appears to have made little impression on Battersea's working classes, who were forced by their impoverished circumstances to spend most of their time thinking of more pressing day to day matters. Yet when the brown dog came into their midst it found ready supporters among the locals – and especially their children, who according to the the Morning Leader of 21 November 1907, regarded the dog as 'a mute friend of long-standing, for they understand each other, if not the dog's mission.'

When Ford first visited the memorial he could not believe how supportive of animal rights the locals had become. 'I had evidently landed in a hotbed of anti-vivisection, where the very boys in the street take up cudgels for the dogs', he said. 'I have many times come across little boys who throw stones at dogs, but the companionship of the Battersea brown dog seemed to have produced a solicitousness for animal welfare only too often absent from the heart of thoughtless boyhood.'

His amazement was compounded when he began to interview a small boy who had showed him to the dog. 'I wouldn't 'ave my Bill cut open alive an' kept in a cage for two months and 'anded over from one cutter to another, no, not if I knows it', said the child. 'And as for them stuck-up chaps who yell and shriek 'cause they wants more *hanimals* to cut up, dad said last night he'd sooner die in peace than have them doctorin' 'im.' Asked whether he wouldn't be grateful for his father to be treated by the doctors when he was ill, he replied: 'Not by them doctors, though. We don't trust them 'ere in Battersea. We've got an 'orspital of our own, where the doctors don't believe in cutting *hanimals* up alive.'

Although the working classes generally appeared to have less interest in anti-vivisectionism than their middle class cousins, some commentators have argued that they nevertheless harboured a latent affinity with vivisected animals, not just because they too were oppressed or that the people running the medical profession were generally the same as those who were oppressing the working class, but because – as Ford's little boy suggested – the poorer sections of society were often also subjected to medical experiments by doctors. In the stormy July 1906 council meeting which agreed to erect the memorial at Latchmere, a number of progressive councillors insisted that 'the poor working man patient' was commonly practised on and sometimes harshly treated in hospitals – and that the money paid for treatment was often 'dishonestly' diverted into animal experiments.

Claims that working class women were 'over-operated' on were fairly commonplace in the early part of the century, and feelings against the men of science were often strongest among working class and radically-minded people, as illustrated by the campaign against vaccination. Many of the newspapers with more working class readerships

– such as the Morning Leader, the Star and the Daily News – recognised this, and were generally supportive of the dog.

The BMJ, by contrast, talked with staggering snobbery in its leader of May 9 1903 about the working class recruits to anti-vivisection 'who doubtless find the blood and thunder of the anti-vivisection drama a stimulating addition to the drink, betting and other "wanton indulgences" which, as we have it on the testimony of Mr John Burns, are their natural amusements'.

It is always difficult to unearth historical record of the thoughts of the mass of ordinary people (as opposed to the views of the rich few), but there is no denying that the brown dog did become a class symbol for many, not just in the borough of Battersea but throughout London and the rest of the country.

Geography may also have had its part to play. For the clannish people of Battersea the monument was above all else 'our dog', a symbol of the area they lived in, downtrodden but dignified, an identification point for the outside world and a source of local pride. People knew the place by its memorial and anyone who threatened that memorial also challenged that local identity. It is possible the residents of Latchmere Estate may have adopted it in just the same way whatever it said or signified, although it certainly helped that it was a dog – and it did no harm that it was supported by local politicians who were often working class themselves. Perhaps for this reason the locals were willing to put up with the middle class men and women who came to speak in their grubby corner of the capital, and who, recognising the local pride, praised them for making Battersea what Lind-af-Hageby called 'the most anti-vivisectionist borough in London'

Some chroniclers of the brown dog affair have painted an unrealistically romantic picture of an Edwardian rainbow coalition of local people, women activists and radicals beating away the unjustified attacks of the reactionary establishment. There was less cohesiveness than that. But the link between women, class and the dog was undeniable, and it was defined as much by the medical students and their supporters as by anyone else.

They were quick to identify what they saw as a broad alliance of anti-establishment forces lined up against them in the Latchmere Recreation Ground – and were determined not to give it succour. 'It is regrettable that even a small proportion of Battersea people should have been content to sit hour after hour in the town hall while faddists of all sorts preached their diverse wild doctrines,' said the South Western Star after the protest meetings of January 1908. 'The socialist, the suffragist, the peculiar politician, the religious crank – all took advantage of circumstance and held onto the tail of the little brown dog.'

The link with the suffragettes was thought particularly dangerous – so much so that medical students occasionally extended their disruption of brown dog meetings to cover gatherings of suffragettes. In December 1907 a band of around 100 students from King's College and St Mary's Hospital had invaded a meeting in support of women's suffrage at Paddington Baths, generating a 'crescendo of disorder' during which water jugs, chairs and tables were smashed and one steward had his ear badly torn. 'All who are responsible for the erection of the Battersea structure have every reason to feel ashamed, for it is a monument raised by those who hit below the belt, aided by their ignorant – mostly female – dupes,' said Herbert Sieveking, a consistent opponent of the dog, in the Daily Graphic of 18 September 1906.

To this extent, support for – or opposition to – the dog often depended more on who you preferred to have as allies rather than your specific views on the merits of the anti-vivisectionist cause. Many of the protagonists are likely to have decided to come out in favour of the dog because of those who were ranged against it, and vice versa.

The dog helped fleetingly to unite certain elements of the working classes with suffragettes, trade unionists, socialists and liberals – partly because it occupied the relatively neutral ground of anti-vivisectionism but also because it quite neatly defined the difference between 'them' and 'us'. The diverse groups which rallied around the dog may have had difficulty supporting each other outside the sphere of the recreation ground, but in the dog they had a symbol which brought them into line against a common enemy. It presented them with a rare chance to come together.

It is too easy, though, to paint a simplified picture of those who rallied around the dog – or even of those who opposed it. Although working class trade unionists gave the monument a home, it was bona fide members of the establishment such as Coleridge (who opposed female emancipation), Woodward and Lind-af-Hageby who brought it to life and kept it going – often supported by aristocrats such as Lady Constance Battersea and conservatives such as Sir Frederick Banbury. On the other side of the fence there were figures like Sir Victor Horsley, who was instrumental in getting Bayliss's libel case off the ground but was a strong advocate of women's suffrage and in some ways more broadminded than many of the dog's supporters, such as Lord Llangattock, who spent most of their weekends hunting.

At local government level, too, not everything was black and white: a handful of municipal reformers were generally supportive of the brown dog, while some progressives would have been happy to see it go. John Burns, whose support would have been so valuable, never lent a hand to the memorial, for he did not oppose vivisection. As John Vyvyan suggests in *The Dark Face of Science*, people who agree on the need to stop animal experimentation can often concur on almost nothing else, and are liable to be divided 'not only by class and politics but also by religion, philosophy and theories of therapeutics'.

Given that the brown dog had proved to be such a useful rallying point for people of such disparate views, it is puzzling that its supporters should have allowed themselves to be so easily outmanoeuvred. The hopelessly outnumbered progressives had little leverage after the 1909 elections, but those in the wider anti-vivisectionist movement could surely have found a way of preventing its destruction. Too late, it seems, did Woodward and Lind-af-Hageby wake up to the fact that the municipal reformers could – and would – get rid of it. In the end they spent too much time organising protest meetings and not enough time on the practical realities of how they could stop the monument ending up in the dust destructor. When the borough solicitor began negotiations with Woodward in 1910 she may have been well advised to take the fountain back with a view to re-siting it in the grounds of the Anti-Vivisection Hospital. That way she could have generated more valuable publicity and kept the fountain for a triumphant return when the progressives came back to power in 1912. In the end the anti-vivisectionists underestimated the value of the brown dog as a publicity generator and naively believed that if disappeared they could recreate it if necessary. Coleridge optimistically told the Daily Graphic: 'If the statue were demolished, which is unlikely, it would reappear somewhere else.' He was wrong.

Up to a point that is, for 74 years after the disappearance of the Latchmere Estate fountain there was an interesting sequel to this fascinating story. On 12 December 1985, a new brown dog memorial was unveiled, in Battersea Park, about a quarter of a mile from the old site, by local resident, actor and anti-vivisectionist Geraldine James. Also made of bronze, but this time without the drinking fountain and perched 7ft high on a Portland stone plinth, the new brown dog was an entirely different character, a coquettish, playful looking Jack Russell terrier modelled on Brock, the real life pet of its sculptor Nicola Hicks.

It too had the original controversial inscription, but it also had words of its own, which read: 'This monument replaces the original memorial of the brown dog erected by public subscriptions in Latchmere Recreation Ground, Battersea in 1906. The sufferings of the brown dog at the hands of vivisectors generated much protest and mass demonstrations. It represented the revulsion of the people of London to vivisection and animal experimentation. This new monument is dedicated to the continuing struggle to end these practices. After much controversy the former monument was removed in the early hours of 10 March 1910. This was the result of a decision taken by the then Battersea Metropolitan Borough Council, the previous council having supported the erection of the memorial. Animal experimentation is one of the greatest moral issues of our time and should have no place in a civilised society. In 1903, 19,084 animals suffered and died in British laboratories. During 1984, 3,497,335 animals were burned, blinded, irradiated, poisoned and subjected to countless other horrifying cruel experiments in Great Britain.'

Hicks had been commissioned to create the £6,000 sculpture by the NAVS and the BUAV, who shared most of the cost but launched a joint campaign which raised £1,000 from members of the public. The idea had first been mooted in 1981 by NAVS volunteer Jose Parry, who had been fascinated by the brown dog's story and had vowed to bring it back to life in some form. The idea of a new memorial took four years to reach fruition, but like its predecessor the new monument had found a left-wing political sponsor – this time in the shape of the Labour-controlled Greater London Council, which owned Battersea Park. Conservative-controlled Wandsworth council had to give their permission too, because they were soon to inherit the park with the abolition of the GLC; this they did, though not with any noticeable enthusiasm. Strangely enough, Parry and her friends gave only brief consideration to resurrecting the monument on its original site in Latchmere Recreation Ground, which was still much the same as it had been 75 years before, It was now felt to be too much of a backwater for such a significant piece of work. Most of those involved in the creation of the new monument favoured erecting it on the Thames embankment near the GLC's County Hall – outside of Battersea altogether. But the GLC quashed that idea early on.

It was Tony Banks, chair of the GLC arts and recreation committee and later to become MP for Newham North West, who first intimated that

The new dog: a coquettish contrast to its down-to-earth predecessor

space would be made for the statue in Battersea Park. But it was his successor Peter Pitt who represented the GLC at the unveiling on a bright, cold day in front of around 100 invited guests. Also present was Wandsworth's deputy mayor and a clutch of anti-vivisectionists. The BUAV and NAVS had backed the idea for its 'publicity potential' and they were not disappointed; numerous newspaper articles appeared the following week with photographs of the original dog and lurid tales of the 1907 'riots'. What's more, the controversy over the inscription was revived.

The BMJ, awakened from a lifetime's slumber, once again summoned up all its old indignation, conceding in its 8 March 1986 editorial that 'nothing can legally stop the anti-vivisectionists from reprinting their lies of the early 1900s,' but adding: 'It is amazing, however, that 74 years after the first brown dog memorial was removed and destroyed ... and the inscription excised from the base of the fountain, a public authority, the Greater London Council, should allow the libel to be reincarnated in a public park as one of its last actions before its extinction in a few months. The next authority responsible for Battersea Park should remove this degrading, libellous and offensive memorial.' In a separate development, Tim Biscoe, one of Bayliss's modern day successors as head of physiology at University College, accused The Observer of 'going some way to repeating the libel of Coleridge v Bayliss' in a news report about the unveiling of the second statue.

In anticipation of such rhetoric, and in an echo of the indemnity put forward by Louisa Woodward in 1906, the GLC's solicitors had insisted that NAVS and BUAV should fix up at least one year's worth of libel cover for the new statue at a cost of £2,000, although legal advisers judged the libel risk as 'small' and no court action was forthcoming. The decision to spend so much money on the sculpture did, though, cause rumblings of discontent at the BUAV, where internal papers show the idea the idea of spending so much money was not entirely popular among members of staff. A satirical poster asking if people would prefer to see the dog 'standing, sitting, pissing or mounting' prompted a warning note to staff which hoped that 'in future if anyone has criticisms or suggestions to offer that they will at least ask to hear both sides of the argument before coming to a conclusion.' Internal strife, it added, 'is damaging not only to those involved but to the movement as a whole and it is not inconceivable that our opposition will exploit such situations'.

It is not easy to understand why, after almost 80 years of apathy, the momentum for a second brown dog memorial should have appeared in the 1980s. The Battersea of 1985 was a much-changed place compared with the borough of 1906, and its political representatives were not nearly as inclined to support such gestures as their predecessors. Although still a relatively unfashionable area of the capital with significant levels of unemployment, Battersea no longer centred on the smoke-belching riverside factories of yesteryear, which had by now all-but disappeared. As in other areas of London, gentrification had taken hold – and the social make-up of the area had begun to change. Local government reorganisation had shifted the centre of political power from the narrow confines of Battersea Town Hall (which had become an arts centre) to the wider catchment area of the London Borough of Wandsworth, diluting Battersea's Labour-inclined influence with traditionally Tory areas such as Putney and Roehampton. The expanded borough was controlled by a 'flagship' Conservative council determined to cut back local authority spending and to privatise as many of its functions as possible. Though still hanging onto a Labour MP, Battersea's parliamentary constituency would soon return a Conservative.

It was not, then, any resurgence of interest in Battersea itself which brought forth the second memorial. While the political patronage came this time from a London-wide body in the form of the GLC – a natural 'loony left' successor to the 'faddist' Battersea council run by the progressives – the real impetus for the Hicks statue stemmed from a renewed national interest in anti-vivisectionism. The 1980s were a significant growth period for campaigners in the field, as large numbers of people were drawn to vegetarianism, the green movement and the new sphere of militant animal rights activism.

Although, as in 1906, the new memorial would not have seen the light of day but for a handful of committed individuals, those individuals were encouraged in their venture by a national atmosphere in which the statue became newly relevant, especially as lobbying intensified up to the Animals (Scientific Procedures) Act of 1986, which tinkered with animal experiment licensing procedures and introduced a 'pain v benefit' clause. In 1906 three sets of circumstances had come together to create the first memorial – a catalyst event in the shape of the Bayliss v Coleridge case, the presence of willing backers in the form of the Battersea progressives, and a relatively high background level of interest in vivisection. From 1911 to the 1980s those three factors failed to coincide simultaneously again (certainly not in Battersea). But by the 1980s two of them were again present – the willing backers in the shape of Labour-led GLC and the renewed background level of interest in vivisection. This it seems, was enough to bring the second dog into life.

It was not enough, however, to sustain much interest in the second monument, or to generate the intense controversy which followed its predecessor. The Hicks statue was a memorial to a memorial, once-removed from the context of the original and less provocative as a consequence. Had its inscription attacked something of modern day relevance – the imprisonment of an Animal Liberation Front activist, for instance, or animal experiments at a named pharmaceutical company – then it may well have sparked scenes similar to those of 1907. But it did not, and interested though many people were in its origins, the events it commemorated were too far back in history to generate anything more than the BMJ's cursory disapproval.

In any case, another component of the original brown dog affair was also missing: a mobilised force of angry medical students backed by the medical establishment. BUAV promotions officer Peter Knowles has claimed that this was because modern students were 'no longer against us – they are uniting with us to oppose vivisection'. This may have been partly true, but the more likely explanation is that the medical students of

Nicola Hicks with the new brown dog

1985 felt far less threatened than their counterparts of 1907. Vivisection was in its infancy in Edwardian Britain and the brown dog memorial challenged the medical profession on a vulnerable front. By the 1980s (as the new memorial pointed out) animal experiments were being conducted in their millions, not thousands – and not just in medical establishments. Vivisection was no new concept, it was firmly established. Why, in this context, should medical students feel the need to react?

By the standards of its predecessor the new statue has therefore lived a long, sedate and unruffled life, free from protest meetings and safe from sledgehammers and crowbars. In November 1987 a small group of anti-vivisectionists in Edwardian dress chose it as the venue for a low-key commemoration of the 80th anniversary of the Trafalgar Square disturbances – but it has kept a low profile for most of its life. Except that is, for its disappearance in 1992, when Battersea Park's new owners, Wandsworth council, decided to move the statue from its position by the old pumping house near Queenstown Road and banish it to the back of a dusty shed near the greenhouses next to Albert Bridge Road.

The statue's absence went unnoticed at first, and it had languished in the shed for some time before a campaign for its return gathered pace. Anti-vivisectionists who had helped bring the new statue into life began to suspect the new version was being kept deliberately from the public gaze by an unsympathetic Wandsworth council. Jose Parry, who had become 'incandescent with rage' when she first discovered the dog's disappearance, told the Big Issue in December 1993: 'They keep telling me it will be back in a couple of months, but it's been 18 months now since it was taken away and I'm beginning to get very angry. I hope this is not some sort of covert decision by the council to quietly drop the statue. People come from far and wide to see the brown dog memorial and they are astonished when they find that it has been removed. It's a beautiful statue and it makes an important statement about experiments on animals in a part of London strongly associated with the anti-vivisection movement.'

A Wandsworth council spokeswoman claimed the memorial had been taken down as part of a renovation programme for the pumping house and would be back in March 1994. But, thanks partly to a breakdown of communications between the council and the NAVS, it only reappeared in the second half of 1994, this time repositioned in a secluded woodland area near the park's Old English Garden. It stands there still, slightly off the beaten track (perhaps deliberately so), but a point of interest to those who cut through the trees towards the centre of the park. One day a small incident may spark it into life, mobilising a modern day Lind-af-Hageby or Lister. Or maybe it will just see out its days there, a permanent reminder of a strange affair which caught the imagination of so many.

chronology

1 May 1903 Coleridge mentions brown dog in his speech to NAVS annual meeting at St James's Hall

11 November 1903 Bayliss v Coleridge trial begins

18 November 1903 trial ends; Coleridge ordered to pay £2,000 damages

8 June 1904 International Anti Vivisection Council seeks permission to erect brown dog memorial

11 July 1906 memorial given final go-ahead by Battersea council

15 September 1906 memorial unveiled

20 November 1907 Howard Lister leads attack on memorial, ten arrested

22 November 1907 effigy burning and demonstrations by medical students in central London

10 December 1907 brown dog 'riots' in Trafalgar Square: 12 arrested

11 December 1907 anti-vivisectionist meeting at Acton Central Hall disrupted by medical students

8 January 1908 Battersea council considers letter about expense of policing memorial

10 January 1908 first of three pro-brown dog meetings at Battersea Town Hall

22 January 1908 Battersea council rejects police commissioner's letter

6 February 1908 questions in House of Commons about memorial

1 November 1909 municipal reformers win power in Battersea

8 November 1909 medical student Arthur Allan arrested trying to bribe policeman near memorial

8 December 1909 council votes to change memorial's inscription

9 February 1910 council votes to return memorial to its donors

9 March 1910 council votes to dismantle memorial

10 March 1910 team of workmen take down memorial in early morning

18 March 1910 protest march by brown dog supporters in Trafalgar Square

20 January 1911 Louisa Woodward unsuccessful in court action for return of memorial

23 March 1911 memorial probably destroyed

12 December 1985 new monument unveiled in Battersea Park

mayors of Battersea during the relevant period

1903/4   William Watts
1904/5   Augustus West
1905/6   William Rines
1906/7   James Brown
1907/8   Fred Worthy
1908/9   William Willis
1909/10 Peter Haythornthwaite
1910/11 John Astill
1911/12 Arthur Runeckles
1912/13 Thomas Brogan

bibliography

A Century of Vivisection and Anti-vivisection, E Westacott, C W Daniel & Co, 1949

The Agitation For and Against the Brown Dog Memorial, Margaret Dawson, Battersea Trades and Labour Council annual report, 1907

All Heaven in a Rage, E S Turner, Centaur Press, 1992

An Inner History of the Late Doings at Battersea, William Lister, unpublished manuscript, University College London Library

An Introduction to Battersea's Labour Movement, 1884-1914, Sean Creighton, Battersea & Wandsworth Labour and Social History Group, 1980

Antivivisection and Medical Science in Victorian Society, Richard French, Princeton University Press, 1975

Battersea Boy, Edward Ezard, William Kimber & Co, 1979

Battersea Republicans and the 1902 Coronation, Chris Wrigley, Battersea & Wandsworth Labour & Social History Group, 1977

The Brown Dog Affair, L E Bayliss, unpublished manuscript, University College London Library

The Brown Dog and His Memorial, Edward Ford, Anti-Vivisection Council, 1908.

Charlotte Despard: A Biography, Margaret Mulvihill, Pandora, 1989

The Dark Face of Science, John Vyvyan, Michael Joseph, 1971

Essays in Anti-Labour History, K D Brown, 1974

The Godless Students of Gower Street, David Taylor, University College London Union, 1968

Health with Humanity, Steve McIvor (ed), BUAV, 1990

John Burns, G D H Cole, Fabian Society, 1943

Keeping My Head: The Memoirs of a British Bolshevik, Harry Wicks, Socialist Platform, 1992

London's open air statuary, Lord Edward Gleichen, Longmans, 1928

Metropolitan Borough of Battersea official guide, 4th edition, 1922

The Old Brown Dog, Coral Lansbury, University of Wisconsin Press, 1985

The Shambles of Science, Louise Lind-af-Hageby & Leisa Schartau, Animal Defence & Anti-Vivisection Society, 5th edition, 1915

The Story of Battersea, Ethel Woolmer, Sampson Low, Marston & Co, 1924

The Story of the Battersea Dogs' Home, Gloria Cottesloe, David and Charles, 1979

University College and its Medical school, WR Merrington, Heinnemann, 1976

Victims of Science, Richard Ryder, NAVS, 1983

Vivisection in Historical Perspective, Nicolaas A Rupke, Croom Helm, 1987

William Howard Lister, Walter Seton, Medici Society, 1919

The World of UCL 1828 -1990, Negley Harte and John North, 1978

index

Abolitionist 74
Acton 63, 64, 67
Acton Central Hall 61, 67
Akers Douglas, Aretas, 12
Albert Bridge Road 110
Allan, Arthur 77, 78
Alverstone, Lord 12, 13, 17
Animal Defence & Anti-Vivisection Society 96
Animal experiments 3, 8, 12, 106, 109
Animal Liberation Front 109
Animals (Scientific Procedures) Act 1986 109
Anti-Vivisection Hospital 30, 43, 55, 83, 87, 94, 105
Anti-Vivisection Society of Sweden 8
Archer, John 65, 83
Association for the Advancement of Medicine by Research 60
Astill, John 35, 77, 83, 91, 92
Astor, William 96
Baird, John 64
Banbury, Sir Frederick 12, 104
Banks, Tony 106
Baptist Times, The 20
Baron's Court 51
Battersea 5, 24-28, 30, 46, 49, 51, 54, 59, 76, 79, 82, 101, 103, 108
Battersea Bridge Road 31
Battersea council 24, 27, 33, 43, 44, 60, 64, 71, 72, 73, 75, 80, 83, 85, 87, 88, 90, 92, 106
Battersea Dogs' Home 30, 94
Battersea General Hospital 30, 43, 55, 83, 87, 94, 105
Battersea Labour League 27
Battersea, Lady Constance 24, 104
Battersea Park 24, 29, 59, 105, 107, 110
Battersea Park Road 5, 32, 38, 42, 49, 54, 84
Battersea Polytechnic 30
Battersea Rise 31
Battersea Square 31
Battersea Town Hall 24, 34, 66, 67, 68, 73, 75, 80, 85, 101, 103, 108
Battersea Trades & Labour Council 27, 76, 101
Battersea Vestry 75
Bayliss, Leonard 18, 92
Bayliss, William 11, 12, 14, 15, 16, 17, 18, 20, 22, 32, 41, 94-95
Bell, Ernest 22
Bernard Shaw, George 37
Bigden, Henry 46, 79, 89
Big Issue 111
Birmingham Daily Mail 44
Birmingham Post 20
Biscoe, Tim 107
Boer War 28
Bowley, Alexander 56
Bow Street court 55
Bridge Road West 31
British Medical Journal (BMJ) 10, 12, 20, 30, 44, 58, 61, 73, 98, 100, 103, 107, 109
British Union for the Abolition of Vivisection (BUAV) 21, 22, 24, 106, 107, 108, 109
Brogan, Thomas 76, 82
Brolly, Patrick 76, 82
Brown Dog League 74
Brown, Edie 77, 89
Brown, James 35
Buller, Terence 63
Burdett, Harry 56
Burns, John 25, 28, 29, 75, 103, 105
Burns Road 29, 32, 77
Cambridge University 51, 56
Campbell Bannerman, Sir Henry 27
Canine Defence League 66
Capel, Arthur 68
Cannon Row 52
Carr, George 56
Caudwell, Paul 83
Caxton Hall 64, 67, 96
Central (Unemployed) Body for London 32
Chandos Place 48
Charing Cross Hospital 47
Chelsea 25
Cheltenham Ladies College 7
Chesterton, GK 59

Christian Commonwealth 58
Churchill, Winston 88
Clapham Junction 25, 31
Clarke, Erskine 24
Claypon, Janet 16
Cobbe, Frances 21
Coleridge, Stephen 9, 10, 11, 12, 13, 17, 18, 19, 20, 21, 22, 41, 60, 73, 97, 98, 99, 101, 104, 105
Commissioner of Police 65, 66, 69, 70, 71, 73
Coombes, Harry 56
County & Borough Councils Act 1907 77
County Hall 106
Criterion, The 56
Cruelty to Animals Act 1876 10, 21
Daffern, PC 43
Daily Chronicle 56, 60, 61, 63, 68
Daily Graphic 49, 104, 105
Daily Mail 18, 65, 70, 78
Daily News 12, 18, 19, 21, 57, 58, 96, 103
Daily Telegraph 56, 96
Dale, Henry 14, 95
Dark face of science, The 18
De Meza, Emanuel 50
de Rutzen, Albert 50
Despard, Charlotte 27, 37, 67, 68, 76, 83, 100
Deuntzer, Canute 43
Drinking fountains 23
Drury Lane 74
Dudgeon, Christopher 56
Ealing & Acton Anti-Vivisection Society 61
Ede, Chuter 97
Educational Correspondence College 98
Effigies 47, 49, 50, 56, 61
Ellis, Sergeant 43
Empire Day 28
Empire Theatre 54
Evans, William 89, 91
Eyre, John 82
Ezard, Edward 25
Falcon Road 31, 85
Ford, Edward 38, 48, 56, 70, 74, 98, 100, 102
Foster, Gregory 50
Freedom Street 29
Fuelings, Arthur 50
Fullerton (greyhound) 16
Gladstone, Herbert 69, 70, 71
Golders Hill Park 24
Goodyear, Robert 50
Gotch, Francis 16
Gower Street 47, 101
Grange, Frederick 56
Greater London Council 106, 107, 109
Guy's Hospital 47, 49
Hammersmith Road 51

Hardie, Keir 27
Hardy, Thomas 11
Haythornthwaite, Peter 32, 77, 78, 80, 81, 91, 92
Hendon council 24
Hendon public park 24
Henry, Sir Edward 65, 66, 69, 70, 71, 73
Hicks, Nicola 106, 110
High Court 12, 18, 20, 22, 86, 89
Highways & dustings committee 31, 33, 78, 79 80, 81, 90, 91
Hobday, Frederick 16
Horse Guards Parade 64
Horsley, Sir Victor 12, 104
House of Commons 12, 69
Hume, Douglas 16
Hyde Park 52, 86
Idris, Arthur 43
Illustrated London News 59
Incorporated Parliamentary Association for the Abolition of Vivisection 100
Inscription 23, 73, 78, 79, 81, 82, 88, 90, 106, 107
International Anti-Vivisection Council 23, 33, 34, 37, 78, 80, 81, 82, 88, 92, 94
Irish Crimes Act 70
Irish home rule 28, 57
Isaacs, Rufus 14, 17
James, Geraldine 105
Jeffery, Joseph 37
Jenner statue 83
Jerome, Jerome K 11
Jones, Duncan 42, 43
Joubert Street 29
Kekewich, Sir George 83, 86, 100
Kennel News 13
Kensington 52
Kensington Gardens 83
Keyworth, Arthur 56
King's College 47, 48, 49, 54, 56, 57
Kipling, Rudyard 11
Knowles, Peter 109
Labour Party 98
Lammas Hall 31
Lancet, The 31, 92
Latchmere Estate 29, 31, 32, 37, 38, 42, 43, 49, 54, 55, 87, 88
Latchmere pub 5
Latchmere Recreation Ground 5, 32, 33, 75, 81, 83, 84, 91, 94, 103, 106
Latchmere Road 29
Latchmere swimming baths 29, 82
Lavender Hill 24, 31, 43, 55
Lavender Sweep 31

Law, Hugh *70*
Leffingwell, Albert *99*
Leicester Square *48, 50, 54*
Lind-af-Hageby, Louise *7- 9, 10, 11, 14, 15, 17, 21, 22, 23, 31, 61, 63, 64, 67, 68, 80, 83, 86, 95-96, 99, 100, 103, 104, 105, 111*
Liscombe, Robert *43*
Lister, Howard *42, 43, 46, 47, 51, 54, 64, 95, 111*
Llangattock, Lord *11, 101, 105*
Local Government Chronicle *86*
London Argus *40*
London County Council *24, 26*
London dock strike *26*
London Evening Standard *49, 55*
London School of Medicine for Women *8, 9, 16*
Lowry, Eleanor *16*
MacGillicuddy, Adolf *42, 43*
Magnus, Sir Philip *50, 69, 70*
Malicious Damage to Property Act *77*
Manchester Guardian *64*
Manser, William *89*
Mansfield, William *43*
Marlborough Street court *50*
Martin, Marjorie *91*
McManus, Leonard *79, 81, 82, 99*
Medical Research Defence Society *100*
Metropolitan Drinking Fountain & Cattle Trough Association *24*
Metropolitan Hospital Sunday Fund *43*
Middlebrook, Samuel *50*
Middlesex Hospital *43, 47*
Morning Leader *13, 38, 44, 80, 103*
Morphine *16*
Municipal reformers *27, 34, 46, 66, 73, 75, 81, 82, 84, 86, 89, 91, 92, 93, 105*
Municipal socialism *27*
Mursell, Rev Arthur *100*
National Anti-Vivisection Society (NAVS) *9, 10, 17, 18, 20, 21, 97, 100, 101, 106, 108, 111*
National Gallery *52*
Nelson's Column *52*
Neville, Justice *86, 88*
Nine Elms *27, 76*
Noel, Rev Conrad *37*
Norman, Burford *43*
Northumberland Avenue *52*
Observer, The *20, 108*
Operative Bricklayers Society *66, 101*
Overton, Robert *56*
Oxford Street *48*
Oxford University *16, 51*
Paddington Baths *104*
Paget, James *60*

Paget, Stephen *60, 68, 73*
Pall Mall Gazette *96*
Pantomime *74*
Parker, Ella *16*
Parliament *5, 12, 41, 98, 100*
Parliamentary committee *86*
Parliament Street *64*
Parry, Jose *106, 111*
Pasteur Institute *7, 97*
Petitions *72, 80, 81, 82*
Piccadilly *52*
Piccadilly Circus *50, 54*
Pitt, Peter *107*
Police *42, 43, 46, 48, 54, 55, 63, 70, 77, 79, 84*
Price's Candles *25*
Prince of Wales Drive *31*
Prince's Head pub *85*
Progressives *27, 28, 32, 40, 65, 68, 69, 72, 73, 75, 78, 80, 89, 94, 98, 102, 105, 109*
Public Authorities Act 1898 *10*
Queen's Club *51*
Queenstown Road *110*
Ranson, Joseph *69*
Rees, George *46*
Reform Street *29, 34*
Research Defence Society *68*
Rhys Warburton, Llewellyn *56*
Richards, John *79*
Rines, William *37, 68, 79, 80, 97*
Riot (Damages) Act 1886 *72*
Royal Commission *99*
Royal Institute of Medicine *74*
Runeckles, Arthur *65, 66, 69, 73, 92, 98*
St Bartholomew's Hospital *16*
St Clement Danes Church *48*
St George's Hospital *52*
St James's Hall *10, 12, 17, 21, 101*
St Martin's Lane *54*
St Mary's Hospital *104*
St Paul's School *52*
Saklatvala, Shapurji *27*
Saunders, Edward *43, 44*
Schartau, Leisa *7- 9, 10, 11, 14, 15, 20, 21, 22*
Scott, William *82*
Scuffle, Charles *14*
Seafield, Countess of *37*
Seton, William *95*
Sewell, Alf *16*
Sewell, Dobbs *50*
Sewell, Horace *50*
Shaftesbury Estate *30*
Shaftesbury, Lord *30*
Shambles of Science, The *7, 9, 17, 22, 96*
Shepherd's Bush *63*

Sieveking, Herbert *104*
Simpson, Capt William *24*
Simpson, Frederick *56*
Sloane Street *96*
Smeaton, Donald *70*
Smith, George *34*
Social Democratic Federation *28*
Society for United Prayer for the Prevention of Cruelty to Animals *23*
South London Press *36*
South Western Star *27, 34, 36, 40, 44, 46, 60, 65, 68, 76, 82, 84, 85, 90, 99, 104*
Starling, Ernest *13, 14, 15, 16*
Star, The *19, 58, 95, 103*
Stewards *64, 66, 68, 80, 104*
Stockholm Opera House *7*
Strindberg, August *96*
Subscription funds *18*
Suffragettes *5, 37, 57, 100, 101, 104*
Sun, The *19*
Taylor, Julian *43*
Taylor, Paul *43, 44, 47, 48, 49, 64*
Temperance movement *5, 30, 69*
Thames, River *49, 51, 106*
Theatre Street *76*
Times, The *20, 27, 60, 73, 90, 94*
Titanic Memorial *23*
Tottenham Court Road *42, 47, 48*
Trade unionism *25, 57, 87, 97, 100, 101*
Trafalgar Square *48, 51, 52, 54, 55, 56, 57, 58, 60, 64, 86, 110*
Unemployment *11, 32, 65, 87, 108*
University College, London *10, 11, 12, 13, 18, 22, 23, 33, 34, 40, 41, 43, 47, 49, 50, 51, 60, 70, 72, 74, 88, 94, 95*

University of London *5, 58, 69, 72*
University College Union magazine *44, 58*
Uxbridge Road *63*
Vaccination *28*
Vaccination Act 1898 *28*
Victoria Street Society *21*
Vivisection bill *12*
Vyvyan, John *18, 61, 105*
Walton, Lawson *15*
Wandsworth Borough News *37, 38, 40, 45, 76, 90, 92*
Wandsworth council *106, 108, 110, 111*
Watts, William *28, 81, 85, 97*
Wellcome Trust *95*
West, Augustus *34, 81, 82, 97*
White, Sydney *56*
Whitehall *54*
Whitehead, Joseph *23*
Whitehead, Sidney *56*
Wicks, Harry *25*
Wilberforce, William *27*
Wilde, Oscar *21*
Wilkins, Marcus *46, 81, 83*
Willcox, Stuart *51*
Willis, William *72, 73, 75, 80*
Wilson, Havelock *27*
Woodford, George *16*
Woodward, Louisa *23, 24, 25, 30, 31, 32, 33, 37, 67, 72, 80, 83, 84, 86, 87, 88, 92, 96, 99, 104, 105*
World League Against Vivisection *23, 96*
Yorkshire Herald *50*
Zoopholist *18, 20, 22*